60 Music Quizzes

FOR THEORY & READING

ONE-PAGE REPRODUCIBLE TESTS TO EVALUATE STUDENT MUSICAL SKILLS

Jay Althouse

©2007 by Alfred Publishing Co., Inc.
All Rights Reserved. Printed in USA.

ISBN-10: 0-7390-4398-6
ISBN-13: 978-0-7390-4398-1

Cover Illustration by Charles Grace.

Contents

Contents (cont.)

THE BASICS

Staff,
Notes,
& Rests

Quiz 1

The Musical Staff

DIRECTIONS: Draw a whole note on the line or in the space shown below. One example has been given.

1.
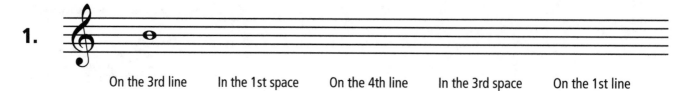

On the 3rd line   In the 1st space   On the 4th line   In the 3rd space   On the 1st line

DIRECTIONS: Draw a half note on the line or in the space shown below. One example has been given.

2.
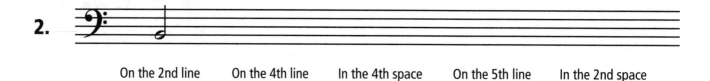

On the 2nd line   On the 4th line   In the 4th space   On the 5th line   In the 2nd space

DIRECTIONS: Draw a quarter note on the line or in the space shown below. One example has been given.

3.

In the 1st space   On the 1st line   In the 3rd space   On the 4th line   In the 4th space

DIRECTIONS: Draw an eighth note on the line or in the space shown below. One example has been given.

4.
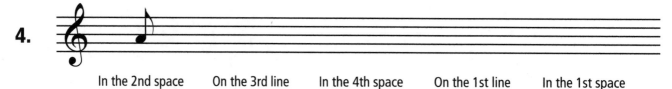

In the 2nd space   On the 3rd line   In the 4th space   On the 1st line   In the 1st space

Name: _____

Class: _____

 # Notes and Rests

DIRECTIONS: What kind of note is it? Circle the correct answer.

1.

Half note

Quarter note

2.

Quarter note

Whole note

3.

Half note

Eighth note

4.

Whole note

Quarter note

DIRECTIONS: What kind of rest is it? Circle the correct answer.

5.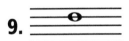

Eighth rest

Quarter rest

6.

Eighth rest

Half rest

7.

Half rest

Whole rest

8.

Half rest

Whole rest

DIRECTIONS: Where is the note on the staff? Circle the correct answer.

9.

4th line

2nd line

10.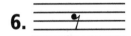

2nd space

2nd line

11.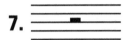

5th line

1st line

12.

2nd space

3rd space

DIRECTIONS: Which clef is it? Circle the correct answer.

13.

Treble Clef

Bass Clef

Alto Clef

14.

Treble Clef

Bass Clef

Alto Clef

Name: _____

Class: _____

Quiz 3 # Know Your Notes and Rests

DIRECTIONS: Name each note or rest. Write the correct letter from the second column in the blank space.

1. ____

2. ____

3. ____

4. ____

5. ____

6. ____

7. ____

8. ____

A. Eighth Note

B. Eighth Rest

C. Quarter Note

D. Quarter Rest

E. Half Note

F. Half Rest

G. Whole Note

H. Whole Rest

DIRECTIONS: The arrow points to a part of a note. Name that part of the note. Write the correct letter from the second column in the blank space.

9. ____

10. ____

11. ____

12. ____

I. Stem

J. Beam

K. Notehead

L. Flag

Name: _____

Class: _____

 **Note Values**

DIRECTIONS: True or false? Circle the correct answer for each example.

1. ♩ + ♩ = 𝅝   True   False

2. ♩ + ♩ = ♩   True   False

3. ♪ + ♪ = ♩   True   False

4. ♩ + ♩ + ♩ = ♩   True   False

5. ♩ + ♩ = ♩.   True   False

6. ♩ + ♩ + ♩ = 𝅝   True   False

7. ♩ + ♪ = ♩.   True   False

8. ♩ + ♩ + ♩ = 𝅝   True   False

9. ♪ + ♪ + ♩ = ♩.   True   False

10. ♪ + ♪ + ♪ + ♪ = ♩   True   False

Name: _____

Class: _____

Rest Values

DIRECTIONS: True or false? Circle the correct answer for each example.

1. 𝄽 + ▬ = ▬   True   False

2. 𝄾 + 𝄾 = 𝄽   True   False

3. 𝄽 + 𝄽 + 𝄽 + 𝄽 = ▬   True   False

4. 𝄾 + 𝄾 + 𝄾 + 𝄾 = ▬   True   False

5. 𝄽 + 𝄽 = 𝄽·   True   False

6. 𝄽 + ▬ = ▬   True   False

7. 𝄽 + 𝄽 = ▬   True   False

8. 𝄾 + 𝄾 + 𝄾 = 𝄽   True   False

9. ▬ + 𝄽 + 𝄽 = ▬   True   False

10. 𝄽 + 𝄾 = 𝄽·   True   False

Quiz 6

Note and Rest Values

DIRECTIONS: True or false? Are the number of beats in the first example equal to the number of beats in the second example? Circle the correct answer.

1.   True   False

2.   True   False

3.   True   False

4.    True   False

5.   True   False

6.   True   False

7.   True   False

8. 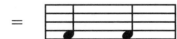   True   False

9.   True   False

10.   True   False

Name: _____

Class: _____

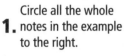 **Identifying Notes**

1. Circle all the whole notes in the example to the right.

2. Circle all the whole notes in the example to the right.

3. Circle all the half notes in the example to the right.

4. Circle all the half notes in the example to the right.

5. Circle all the quarter notes in the example to the right.

6. Circle all the quarter notes in the example to the right.

7. Circle all the eighth notes in the example to the right.

8. Circle all the eighth notes in the example to the right.

THE BASICS

 Quiz

Identifying Rests

1. Circle all the whole rests in the example to the right.

2. Circle all the whole rests in the example to the right.

3. Circle all the half rests in the example to the right.

4. Circle all the half rests in the example to the right.

5. Circle all the quarter rests in the example to the right.

6. Circle all the quarter rests in the example to the right.

7. Circle all the eighth rests in the example to the right.

8. Circle all the eighth rests in the example to the right.

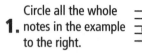

Identifying Notes and Rests

1. Circle all the whole notes in the example to the right.

2. Circle all the half notes in the example to the right.

3. Circle all the quarter notes in the example to the right.

4. Circle all the eighth notes in the example to the right.

5. Circle all the whole rests in the example to the right.

6. Circle all the half rests in the example to the right.

7. Circle all the quarter rests in the example to the right.

8. Circle all the eighth rests in the example to the right.

Name: _____

Class: _____

Notes and Rests Math

DIRECTIONS: In each of the pairs of examples below, one example is correct and one is incorrect. Circle the letter of each example that is correct.

1. A. ♩ + ♩ = 𝅝   or   B. 𝅝 + 𝅝 = ♩

2. A. ♩ + ♩ + ♩ = ♩.   or   B. ♩ + ♩. = ♩

3. A. ♪ + ♪ + ♪ = 𝅝   or   B. ♪ + ♪ + ♪ + ♪ = ♩

4. A. ♩ + ♩ = ♩   or   B. ♩ + ♩ = ♩

5. A. 𝅝 + ♩ = ♩.   or   B. ♩. + ♩ = 𝅝

6. A. ♩ + ♩ = ♩.   or   B. ♩ + ♩ + ♩ = ♩.

7. A. ♪ + ♪ = ♩   or   B. ♩ + ♩ = ♪

8. A. ♩ + ♩ = ♩.   or   B. ♩ + ♩ + ♩ = ♩.

9. A. ♩. + ♩ = 𝅝   or   B. ♪ + ♩ + ♩ = 𝅝

10. A. ♩ + ♩ + ♩ = ♩.   or   B. ♩ + ♩ + ♩ + = 𝅝

11. A. ♪ + ♩ = ♩.   or   B. 𝅝 + ♩ = ♩.

12. A. ♪ + ♪ + ♪ + ♪ = 𝅝   or   B. ♩ + ♩ + ♩ = 𝅝

Quiz 11

Do You Know Your Notes and Rests?

DIRECTIONS: The left example has one note in the staff. In the blank staff to the right, draw two notes which equal the note in the left example.

1. 𝅝 =

3. ♩ =

2. 𝅗𝅥 =

DIRECTIONS: The left example has one rest in the staff. In the blank staff to the right, draw two rests which equal the rest in the left example.

4. ▬ =

6. 𝄽 =

5. ▬ =

DIRECTIONS: The left example has one note in the staff. In the blank staff to the right, draw four notes which equal the note in the left example.

7. 𝅝 =

8. 𝅗𝅥 =

DIRECTIONS: The left example has one rest in the staff. In the blank staff to the right, draw four rests which equal the rest in the left example.

9. ▬ =

10. ▬ =

RHYTHM

Name: _____

Class: _____

How Many Quarter Note Beats in a Measure?

DIRECTIONS: If a quarter note gets one beat, how many beats are there in the meaure? Write the correct answer in the space.

1. _____

2. _____

3. _____

4. _____

5. _____

6. _____

7. _____

8. _____

9. _____

10. _____

11. _____

12. _____

13. _____

14. _____

RHYTHM

Quiz 13

How Many Half and Eighth Note Beats in a Measure?

DIRECTIONS: If a half note gets one beat, how many beats are there in the meaure? Write the correct answer in the space.

1. _____

2. _____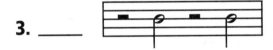

3. _____

4. _____

5. _____

6. _____

DIRECTIONS: If an eighth note gets one beat, how many beats are there in the meaure? Write the correct answer in the space.

7. _____

8. _____

9. _____

10. _____

11. _____

12. _____

13. _____

14. _____

Name: _____

Class: _____

Quiz **14**

Barlines and Measures— Quarter Note Beat

DIRECTIONS: In the examples below, a quarter note gets one beat.

In examples 1, 2, and 3, draw barlines after every four beats.

1.

2.

3.

In examples 4, 5, and 6, draw barlines after every three beats.

4.

5.

6.

In examples 7 and 8, draw barlines after every two beats.

7.

8.

RHYTHM

Barlines and Measures—
Half and Eighth Note Beat

DIRECTIONS: In examples 1–4 below, a half note gets one beat.

In examples 1 and 2, draw barlines after every three beats.

1.

2.

In examples 3 and 4, draw barlines after every two beats.

3.

4.

DIRECTIONS: In examples 5–8 below, an eighth note gets one beat.

In examples 5 and 6, draw barlines after every six beats.

5.

6.

In example 7, draw barlines after every four beats.

7.

In example 8, draw barlines after every three beats.

8.

Quiz 16 — Dotted Notes

Name: _____

Class: _____

DIRECTIONS: Write the correct note in each space to complete these musical equations.

1. o = 𝅗𝅥. + _____

2. 𝅗𝅥 = ♩. + _____

3. ♩. = ♩ + _____

4. 𝅗𝅥. = ♩ + ♩ + _____

5. ♩. = ♪ + ♪ + _____

6. o = ♩. + ♪ + _____

DIRECTIONS: In the box, draw one dotted note to complete the measure.

7. [bass clef, 4/4]

8. [treble clef, 6/8]

DIRECTIONS: Place barlines in the correct places in these musical examples.

9. [treble clef, 3/4]

10. [treble clef, 4/4]

DIRECTIONS: In the example below, one measure has too many beats. Draw an **X** over that measure.

11. [bass clef, 2/4]

DIRECTIONS: In the example below, one measure does not have enough beats. Draw an **X** over the measure.

12. [treble clef, 4/4]

Counting Beats in a Measure I

DIRECTIONS: In each of the examples below, one measure does not have enough beats. Draw an **X** over the measure that does not have enough beats.

Name: _____

Class: _____

Quiz 18

Counting Beats in a Measure II

DIRECTIONS: In each of the examples below, one measure has too many beats. Draw an **X** over the measure that has too many beats.

Add the Missing Note

DIRECTIONS: One note is missing in each measure. Write one note in each box to complete the measure. Put the note on any line or in any space. (Remember, the time signature will tell you how many beats are in each measure, and what note gets a beat.)

1.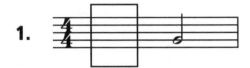

2.

3.

4.

5.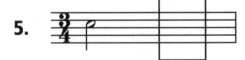

6.

7.

8.

9.

10.

11.

12.

13.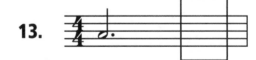

14.

15.

16.

Quiz 20 — Add the Missing Rest

Name: _____

Class: _____

DIRECTIONS: One rest is missing in each measure. Write one rest in each box to complete the measure. (Remember, the time signature will tell you how many beats are in each measure, and what note gets a beat.)

1.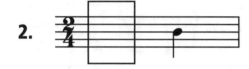

2.

3.

4.

5.

6.

7.

8. (notes on staff)

9.

10.

11.

12.

13.

14.

15.

16. (notes on staff)

Name: _____

Class: _____

quiz 21 Tied Notes

DIRECTIONS: To figure out the value of the two tied notes, add the value of both notes. Are the following musical examples correct? Circle True or False.

1. ♩ ♩ = ♩   True   False   5. ♪ ♪ = ♩   True   False

2. ♩ ♩ = ♪   True   False   6. ♩ ♩ = 𝅝   True   False

3. ♩ ♩ = ♩.   True   False   7. ♩ ♪ = ♩.   True   False

4. ♩ ♩. = 𝅝   True   False   8. 𝅝 𝅝 = ♩   True   False

DIRECTIONS: In the blank space, draw the note or dotted note that equals the two tied notes.

9. ♩. ♩ = ____   11. ♪ ♪ = ____

10. ♩. ♪ = ____   12. ♩ ♩ = ____

DIRECTIONS: In the blank space, draw the correct note or dotted note to the tied note to complete the musical equation.

13. ♩ = ♩. ____   15. ♩ = ♪ ____

14. ♩ = ♩ ____   16. 𝅝 = ♩ ____

Name: _____

Class: _____

Quiz 22 — Musical Equations

DIRECTIONS: These questions will test your knowledge of note values. Write a number in the blank which completes the musical equation.

1. ♪ x ____ = ♩

5. ♩ x ____ = 𝅝

2. ♪ x ____ = ♩

6. ♫ x ____ = ♩

3. ♩ x ____ = 𝅝

7. ♩ x ____ = ♩

4. ♬ x ____ = ♩

8. ♪ x ____ = 𝅝

DIRECTIONS: In the blanks space below, draw one note equal to the value of the notes in the musical equation. You may use dotted notes.

9. ♫ + ♩ = ____

17. ♪ + ♩ + ♪ = ____

10. ♩ + ♩ + ♩ = ____

18. ♬ + ♩ = ____

11. ♬ + ♩ = ____

19. ♫ + ♩. = ____

12. ♩ + ♩ + ♩ = ____

20. ♫ + ♬ + ♩ = ____

13. ♫ + ♬ = ____

21. ♫ + ♩ + ♩ = ____

14. ♬ + ♬ = ____

22. ♩ + ♫ + ♩ = ____

15. ♩ + ♩ + ♩ = ____

23. ♫ + ♫ = ____

16. ♩ + ♫ + ♩ = ____

24. ♪ + ♫ = ____

NOTE NAMES

Name: _____

Class: _____

Note Names – Treble Clef

DIRECTIONS: Write the correct letter name under each note in the treble clef.

DIRECTIONS: Draw quarter notes in the treble clef for each of the following letter names. Don't forget to draw the stem correctly. (Notes below the 3rd line have stems going up. Notes on the 3rd line and above have stems going down.) Do not use ledger lines. In some cases, there may be more than one correct answer.

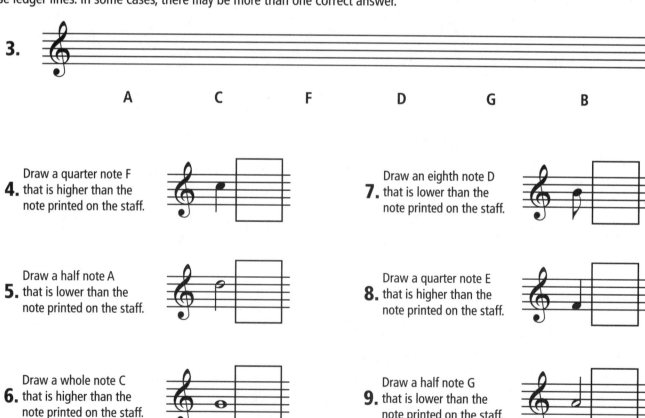

Note Names – Bass Clef

DIRECTIONS: Write the correct letter name under each note in the bass clef.

1.

2.

DIRECTIONS: Draw quarter notes in the bass clef for each of the following letter names. Don't forget to draw the stem correctly. (Notes below the 3rd line have stems going up. Notes on the 3rd line and above have stems going down.) Do not use ledger lines. In some cases, there may be more than one correct answer.

3.

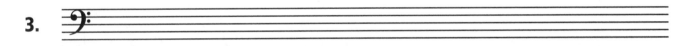

G   A   C   F   B   D

4. Draw a quarter note B that is higher than the note printed on the staff.

7. Draw a whole note G that is lower than the note printed on the staff.

5. Draw a half note C that is lower than the note printed on the staff.

8. Draw an eighth note A that is higher than the note printed on the staff.

6. Draw a quarter note F that is higher than the note printed on the staff.

9. Draw a whole note E that is lower than the note printed on the staff.

Name: _____

Class: _____

Ledger Lines

DIRECTIONS: Write the correct letter name under each note in the treble clef.

1.

_____   _____   _____   _____

DIRECTIONS: Write the correct letter name under each note in the bass clef.

2.

_____   _____   _____   _____

DIRECTIONS: Use ledger lines to draw the correct notes in the boxes.

3. This is a half note A. To its right, draw another half note A above the staff.

5. Now draw a half note A below the staff.

4. This is a whole note D. To its right, draw another whole note D below the staff.

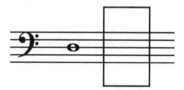

6. Now draw a whole note D above the staff.

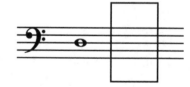

DIRECTIONS: Circle the correct note for the questions below.

7. Which note is a B?

9. Which note is a C?

8. Which note is a G?

10. Which note is an F?

Name: _____

Class: _____

 **Quiz 26**

Sharps and Flats – Treble Clef

DIRECTIONS: Write the correct note name under each note in the treble clef.

1.

_____ _____ _____ _____ _____ _____

2.

_____ _____ _____ _____ _____ _____

DIRECTIONS: Circle the note which is higher.

3.    **4.**    **5.**

DIRECTIONS: Circle the note which is lower.

6.    **7.**    **8.**

DIRECTIONS: Using quarter notes and accidentals, draw the following notes in the treble clef. Do not use ledger lines.
Note: There may be more than one correct answer.

9.

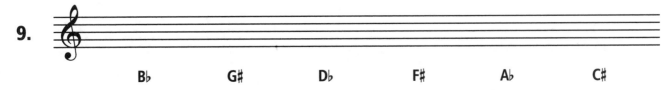

B♭   G♯   D♭   F♯   A♭   C♯

DIRECTIONS: Using half notes and accidentals, draw the following notes in the treble clef. Do not use ledger lines.
Note: There may be more than one correct answer.

10.

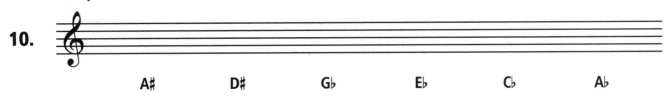

A♯   D♯   G♭   E♭   C♭   A♭

Name: _____

Class: _____

Sharps and Flats – Bass Clef

DIRECTIONS: Write the correct note name under each note in the bass clef.

1.

2.

DIRECTIONS: Circle the note which is higher.

3. **4.** **5.**

DIRECTIONS: Circle the note which is lower.

6. **7.** **8.**

DIRECTIONS: Using quarter notes and accidentals, draw the following notes in the bass clef. Do not use ledger lines. Note: There may be more than one correct answer.

9.

B♭   F♯   C♯   D♯   B♯   G♭

DIRECTIONS: Using half notes and accidentals, draw the following notes in the bass clef. Do not use ledger lines. Note: There may be more than one correct answer.

10.

A♭   E♭   G♯   D♭   F♭   C♭

Name: _____

Class: _____

Quiz 28 — Sharps and Flats – Two Clefs

DIRECTIONS: Write the correct note name under each note in the treble clef.

1.

2.

DIRECTIONS: Circle the note which is higher.

3.    4.    5.

DIRECTIONS: Circle the note which is lower.

6.    7.    8.

DIRECTIONS: Using quarter notes and accidentals, draw the following notes in the treble clef. Do not use ledger lines.
Note: There may be more than one correct answer.

9.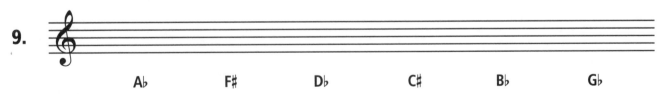

     A♭   F♯   D♭   C♯   B♭   G♭

DIRECTIONS: Using half notes and accidentals, draw the following notes in the bass clef. Do not use ledger lines.
Note: There may be more than one correct answer.

10.

     B♭   G♯   E♭   D♯   F♯   A♭

Quiz 29

Identifying Notes in the Treble Clef

DIRECTIONS: Circle every note that is a G.

1.

DIRECTIONS: Circle every note that is an F.

2.

DIRECTIONS: Circle every note that is an A.

3.

DIRECTIONS: Circle every note that is a B.

4.

DIRECTIONS: Circle every note that is an E.

5.

DIRECTIONS: Circle every note that is a C.

6.

DIRECTIONS: Circle every note that is a D.

7.

DIRECTIONS: Circle every note that is an F.

8.

Name: _____

Class: _____

Identifying Notes in the Bass Clef

DIRECTIONS: Circle every note that is an F.

1.

DIRECTIONS: Circle every note that is a G.

2.

DIRECTIONS: Circle every note that is a C.

3.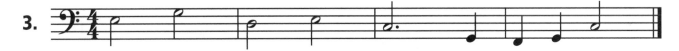

DIRECTIONS: Circle every note that is a D.

4.

DIRECTIONS: Circle every note that is a B.

5.

DIRECTIONS: Circle every note that is an A.

6.

DIRECTIONS: Circle every note that is an E.

7.

DIRECTIONS: Circle every note that is a G.

8.

Name: _____

Class: _____

Quiz 31

Match the Notes – Treble Clef

DIRECTIONS: What is the name of each note? Write the correct answer from the second column in the space.

1. _____   A

2. _____   B♭

3. _____   C

4. _____   D♯

5. _____   E

6. _____   F♯

7. _____   G♭

8. _____   D

9. _____   E♭

10. _____   A♭

Quiz 32   Match the Notes –Bass Clef

DIRECTIONS: What is the name of each note? Write the correct answer from the second column in the space.

1. _____   Ab

2. _____   B

3. _____   C#

4. _____   D

5. _____   Eb

6. _____   F

7. _____   G#

8. _____   Cb

9. _____   E

10. _____   F#

Name: _____

Class: _____

Quiz **33**

Note Names – Treble and Bass Clef

DIRECTIONS: Draw an **X** over any note that is not an F.

1.

DIRECTIONS: Directions: Draw an **X** over any note that is not an A.

2.

DIRECTIONS: Directions: Draw an **X** over any note that is not an E.

3.

DIRECTIONS: Directions: Draw an **X** over any note that is not a D.

4.

DIRECTIONS: In the following examples, draw an **X** over the measure that does not have two notes with the same letter name.

5.

6.

DIRECTIONS: True or False? Are the notes the same? Circle **T** or **F**.

7. = T F   9. = T F

8. = T F   10. = T F

NOTE NAMES

Know Your Notes in Two Clefs

DIRECTIONS: In each example below, draw an **X** over the measure that does not have three notes with the same letter name.

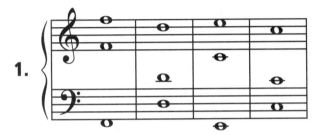
1.

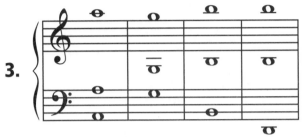
3.

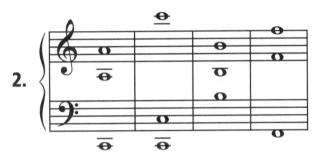
2.

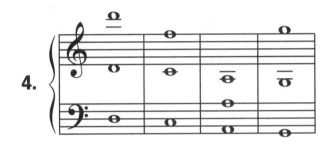
4.

DIRECTIONS: In the box following each whole note, draw another whole note with the same letter name. The note may be in the space above or below the staff, but do not use ledger lines.

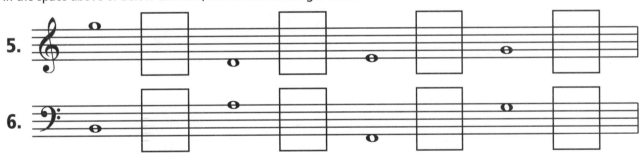
5.

6.

DIRECTIONS: In the following two examples, a whole note is shown in the treble clef. In the blank bass clef, draw a whole note that has the letter name as the note shown in the treble clef. Do not use ledger lines. NOTE: There may be more than one correct answer.

7.

8.

DIRECTIONS: In the following two examples, a whole note is shown in the bass clef. In the blank treble clef, draw a whole note that has the letter name as the note shown in the treble clef. Do not use ledger lines. NOTE: There may be more than one correct answer.

9.

10.

KEY SIGNATURES

Name: _____

Class: _____

Major Key Signatures in the Treble Clef

DIRECTIONS: Write the correct name of each major key signature on the line provided.

1.  ____

4.  ____

7.  ____

2.  ____

5. ____

8.  ____

3. ____

6. ____

9. ____

DIRECTIONS: In the box, write the correct sharps for the following sharp key signatures.

10. 
Key of G

11. 
Key of A

12. 
Key of D

DIRECTIONS: In the box, write the correct flats for the following flat key signatures.

13. 
Key of B♭

14. 
Key of F

15.
Key of A♭

Major Key Signatures in the Bass Clef

Name: _____

Class: _____

DIRECTIONS: Write the correct name of each major key signature on the line provided.

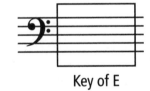

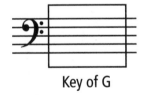

1. _____   4. _____   7. _____

2. _____   5. _____   8. _____

3. _____   6. _____   9. _____

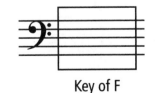

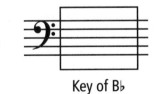

DIRECTIONS: In the box, write the correct sharps for the following sharp key signatures.

10.   11.   12.

Key of D   Key of E   Key of G

DIRECTIONS: In the box, write the correct flats for the following flat key signatures.

13.   14.   15.

Key of E♭   Key of F   Key of B♭

Name: _____

Class: _____

Quiz 37

Major Key Signatures in Treble and Bass Clefs

DIRECTIONS: Write the correct name of each major key signature on the line provided.

1.   ___

2.   ___

3.   ___

4.   ___

5.   ___

6.   ___

7.   ___

8.   ___

9.   ___

DIRECTIONS: In the box, write the correct sharps for the following sharp key signatures.

10.   Key of E

11.   Key of D

12.   Key of G

DIRECTIONS: In the box, write the correct flats for the following flat key signatures.

13.   Key of B♭

14.   Key of A♭

15.   Key of F

Name: _____

Class: _____

Know Your Key Signatures

DIRECTIONS: Find the correct key signature in the second column and write it in the blank space.

1. _____   D

2. _____   F

3. _____   B♭

4. _____   A

5. _____   G

6. _____   E♭

7. _____   A♭

8. _____   E

DIRECTIONS: Find the correct key signature in the second column and write it in the blank space.

9. _____   F

10. _____   D

11. _____   B♭

12. _____   E♭

13. _____   A

14. _____   E

15. _____   G

16. _____   A♭

Name: _____

Class: _____

Quiz 39

Note Naming with Key Signatures and Accidentals – Treble Clef

DIRECTIONS: What is the letter name of the note in the box? Write the correct answer in the blank space.

1.  _____

2.  _____

3.  _____

4.  _____

5.  _____

6.  _____

7.  _____

8.  _____

9.  _____

10.  _____

DIRECTIONS: Using half notes and accidentals, draw the following notes in the treble clef. Do not use ledger lines. Note: There may be more than one correct answer.

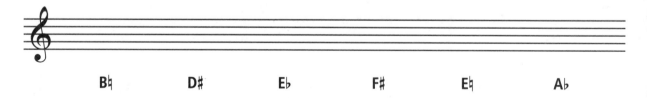

B♮   D#   E♭   F#   E♮   A♭

DIRECTIONS: Using whole notes and accidentals, draw the following notes in the treble clef. Do not use ledger lines. Note: There may be more than one correct answer.

C♭   G#   D♮   A♮   F♮   D♭

Quiz 40

Note Naming with Key Signatures and Accidentals – Bass Clef

DIRECTIONS: What is the letter name of the note in the box? Write the correct answer in the blank space.

1.  _____

6. 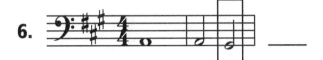 _____

2.  _____

7.  _____

3.  _____

8.  _____

4.  _____

9.  _____

5.  _____

10.  _____

DIRECTIONS: Using quarter notes and accidentals, draw the following notes in the bass clef. Do not use ledger lines.
Note: There may be more than one correct answer.

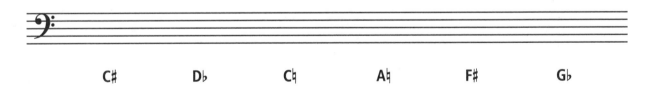

C♯   D♭   C♮   A♮   F♯   G♭

DIRECTIONS: Using half notes and accidentals, draw the following notes in the bass clef. Do not use ledger lines.
Note: There may be more than one correct answer.

B♭   E♭   D♭   G♯   D♮   E♮

Name: _____

Class: _____

Quiz 11

Accidentals in Treble and Bass Clefs

DIRECTIONS: What is the letter name of the note in the box? Write the correct answer in the blank space.

1.  ____

6.  ____

2.  ____

7.  ____

3.  ____

8.  ____

4.  ____

9.  ____

5.  ____

10. ____

DIRECTIONS: Using half notes and accidentals, draw the following notes in the treble clef. Do not use ledger lines.
Note: There may be more than one correct answer.

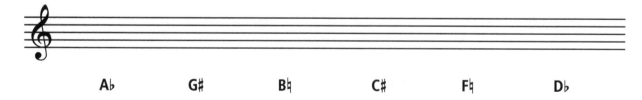

      Ab   G#   B♮   C#   F♮   Db

DIRECTIONS: Using whole notes and accidentals, draw the following notes in the bass clef. Do not use ledger lines.
Note: There may be more than one correct answer.

      E♮   Cb   D#   F#   Bb   G#

MUSICAL SYMBOLS AND TERMS

Name: _____

Class: _____

Know Your Musical Symbols

DIRECTIONS: Name each musical symbol. Write the correct letter from the second column in the blank space.

1. _____ ♭

A. Quarter Note

2. _____

B. Natural

3. _____

C. Treble Clef

4. _____

D. Whole Note

5. _____

E. Staff

6. _____

F. Whole Rest

7. _____

G. Eighth Note

8. _____

H. Sharp

9. _____ o

I. Eighth Rest

10. _____

J. Time Signature

11. _____

K. Half Rest

12. _____

L. Bass Clef

13. _____

M. Flat

14. _____

N. Half Note

15. _____

O. Quarter Rest

Name: _____

Class: _____

Quiz 43 Match the Musical Symbols and Terms

DIRECTIONS: Name each musical symbol. Write the correct letter from the second column in the blank space.

1. _____

A. Tenuto mark

2. _____

B. Marcato

3. _____

C. Accent

4. _____

D. To speed up

5. _____

E. Breath mark

6. _____

F. First ending

7. _____

G. Decrescendo

8. _____

H. Fermata

9. _____

I. To slow down

10. _____

J. Crescendo

11. _____

K. Staccato mark

12. _____

L. Caesura (to pause)

13. _____ *rit.*

M. Coda

14. _____ *accel.*

N. Barline

15. _____

O. Repeat sign

Name: _____

Class: _____

Which Is It? Musical Symbols

DIRECTIONS: Which is it? Circle the letter of the correct answer for each example.

1. $\frac{3}{4}$ This is a   **A.** Time Signature   **B.** Key Signature

2. ▬   This is a   **A.** Whole Rest   **B.** Half Rest

3. 𝅝   This is a   **A.** Half Note   **B.** Whole Note

4. 𝅘𝅥𝅮   These are   **A.** Quarter Notes   **B.** Eighth Notes

5. ⌢   This is a   **A.** Fermata   **B.** Tie

6. ♭   This is a   **A.** Sharp   **B.** Flat

7. 𝄢   This is a   **A.** Bass clef sign   **B.** Treble clef sign

8. ♯   This is a   **A.** Natural   **B.** Sharp

9. 𝄽   This is a   **A.** Half Rest   **B.** Quarter Rest

10. *p*   This means   **A.** Loud   **B.** Soft

11. *rit.*   This means   **A.** Get faster   **B.** Get slower

12. ◁   This means   **A.** Get louder   **B.** Get softer

13. >   This is an   **A.** Eighth Rest   **B.** Accent

14. 𝄇   This means   **A.** Stop playing   **B.** Repeat the section

15.   This dot means   **A.** The note is short   **B.** The note is long

Name: _____

Class: _____

Quiz 45   How Loud? How Soft? Dynamics

DIRECTIONS: Which dynamic level is louder? Circle the correct answer.

1. *p*   or   *mp*   3. *f*   or   *p*

2. *ff*   or   *pp*   4. *mf*   or   *mp*

DIRECTIONS: Which dynamic level is softer? Circle the correct answer.

5. *p*   or   *f*   7. *ff*   or   *f*

6. *mp*   or   *mf*   8. *f*   or   *mp*

DIRECTIONS: What does each dynamic level mean? Write the correct letter from the second column in the blank space.

9. _____ *p*   **A.** Loud

10. _____ *mf*   **B.** Very soft

11. _____ *ff*   **C.** Medium loud

12. _____ *mp*   **D.** Medium soft

13. _____ *f*   **E.** Very loud

14. _____ *pp*   **F.** Soft

DIRECTIONS: Match the Italian term with each dynamic level. Write the correct letter from the second column in the blank space.

15. _____ *p*   **A.** *pianissimo*

16. _____ *mf*   **B.** *piano*

17. _____ *ff*   **C.** *mezzo piano*

18. _____ *mp*   **D.** *mezzo forte*

19. _____ *f*   **E.** *forte*

20. _____ *pp*   **F.** *fortissimo*

Name: _____

Class: _____

Quiz 46

Know Your Musical Dynamics

DIRECTIONS: Write the letter of the correct answer in the blank space.

1. *Decrescendo* means the same as _____

    A. *Diminuendo*

    B. *Crescendo*

2. ◁━━━ means _____

    A. to gradually get louder

    B. to gradually get softer

DIRECTIONS: In the examples below, are the dynamics correct or incorrect? Circle the correct answer.

1.

    Correct   or   **Incorrect**

2.

    Correct   or   **Incorrect**

3.

    Correct   or   **Incorrect**

4.

    Correct   or   **Incorrect**

DIRECTIONS: How loud or soft is the music at Ⓐ, Ⓑ, Ⓒ and Ⓓ? Circle the correct answer.

5.

Ⓐ **Soft**   or   **Loud**   Ⓒ **Very soft**   or   **Medium soft**

Ⓑ **Medium loud**   or   **Medium Soft**   Ⓓ **Very loud**   or   **Very Soft**

Name: _____

Class: _____

 Quiz 47

How Fast? How Slow? Tempo

DIRECTIONS: Which tempo marking is faster? Circle the correct answer.

1. *Largo*   or   *Presto*   3. *Vivace*   or   *Adagio*

2. *Moderato*   or   *Vivace*   4. *Andante*   or   *Allegro*

DIRECTIONS: Which tempo marking is slower? Circle the correct answer.

5. *Presto*   or   *Andante*   7. *Moderato*   or   *Vivace*

6. *Adagio*   or   *Presto*   8. *Andante*   or   *Largo*

DIRECTIONS: What does each tempo marking mean? Write the correct letter from the second column in the blank space.

9. _____ *Allegro*   **A.** Fast

10. _____ *Vivace*   **B.** Very slow

11. _____ *Andante*   **C.** Walking tempo

12. _____ *Largo*   **D.** A moderate speed

13. _____ *Moderato*   **E.** Very fast

14. _____ *Adagio*   **F.** Slow

DIRECTIONS: What does each tempo change mean? Write the correct letter from the second column in the blank space.

15. _____ *ritardando*   **A.** gradually slower

16. _____ *accelerando*   **B.** gradually faster

17. _____ *a tempo*   **C.** return to previous tempo

Name: _____

Class: _____

 Quiz 48

Staccato, Accent, Fermata

DIRECTIONS: Which note is shorter? Circle the note which is shorter.

1.   or

3.   or

2.    or

4.    or

DIRECTIONS: Which note is longer? Circle the note which is longer.

5.   or

7.    or

6. (image)   or   (image)

8. (image)   or   (image)

DIRECTIONS: Place a staccato dot on every G♯ in this example. Be sure to position it correctly, either above or below the notehead.

9.

DIRECTIONS: Place a fermata over every half note in this example.

10.

Name: _____

Class: _____

 **Quiz 49**

Dynamics, Accent, Tenuto, Marcato

DIRECTIONS: Which note is louder? Circle the note which is louder.

1.    or

3.    or

2.    or

4.    or

DIRECTIONS: What does each symbol mean? Write the correct letter from the second column in the blank space.

5. _____ ∧   **A.** Loud

6. _____ >   **B.** Louder

7. _____ —   **C.** Loudest

DIRECTIONS: Place an accent (>) above every B♭ in this example.

8.

DIRECTIONS: Place a marcato mark (∧) over every eighth note in this example.

9.

TIME SIGNATURES

Name: _____

Class: _____

Quiz 50 **Time Signatures: 2/4, 3/4, 4/4**

DIRECTIONS: Write the correct time signature in the box. The answer will be 2/4, 3/4, or 4/4.

1.

2.

3.

4.

5.

6.

7.

8.

9.

10.

Name: _____

Class: _____

More Time Signatures: 2/4, 3/4, 4/4

DIRECTIONS: Write the correct time signature in the box. The answer will be 2/4, 3/4, or 4/4.

1.

2.

3.

4.

5.

6.

7.

8.

9.

10.

Name: _____

Class: _____

Quiz 52 Advanced Time Signatures

DIRECTIONS: Write the correct time signature in the box. The answer will be $\frac{5}{4}$, $\frac{6}{4}$, $\frac{3}{8}$, $\frac{5}{8}$, or $\frac{6}{8}$.

1.

2.

3.

4.

5.

6.

7.

8.

9.

10.

KEYBOARD
IDENTIFICATION

Name: _____

Class: _____

Keyboard Identification – White Notes

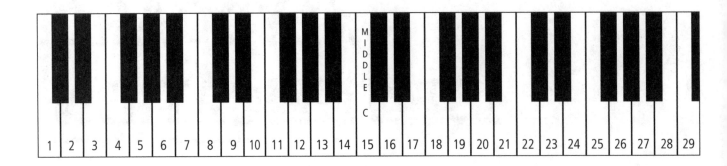

DIRECTIONS: On the line below each note, write the correct number from the keyboard shown above.

1.

___ ___ ___ ___ ___ ___ ___ ___ ___ ___

2.

___ ___ ___ ___ ___ ___ ___ ___ ___ ___

3.

___ ___ ___ ___ ___ ___ ___ ___ ___ ___

4.

___ ___ ___ ___ ___ ___ ___ ___ ___ ___

Name: _____

Class: _____

Keyboard Identification – White and Black Notes

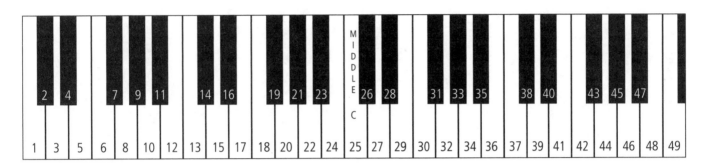

DIRECTIONS: On the line below each note, write the correct number from the keyboard shown above.

1.

2.

3.

4.

MUSICAL PUZZLES

Name: _____

Class: _____

Unscramble the Musical Terms

DIRECTIONS: The left column contains musical terms. The right column contains scrambled words. Unscramble the words in the right column and match them with the musical terms in the left column. Place the correct letter from the right column in the blank space.

1. _____	accent		**A.**	ftafs
2. _____	pianissimo		**B.**	labenir
3. _____	flat		**C.**	spsaiminio
4. _____	tie		**D.**	parhs
5. _____	piano		**E.**	meartfa
6. _____	forte		**F.**	rsdceceoedn
7. _____	marcato		**G.**	eti
8. _____	tempo		**H.**	felc
9. _____	clef		**I.**	poemt
10. _____	natural		**J.**	sremuea
11. _____	staff		**K.**	alnutra
12. _____	tenuto		**L.**	rofet
13. _____	fortissimo		**M.**	ceatcn
14. _____	crescendo		**N.**	anoip
15. _____	barline		**O.**	sifromotsi
16. _____	fermata		**P.**	acsotatc
17. _____	decrescendo		**Q.**	falt
18. _____	staccato		**R.**	eodecscrn
19. _____	measure		**S.**	taormca
20. _____	sharp		**T.**	utneot

Quiz 56 Musical Terms in English

Name: _____

Class: _____

DIRECTIONS: Find the 16 words below in the grid. The words in the grid may be forward, backward, down, up, or diagonal. Each word will always be in a straight line. When you find the word, circle the letters.

```
E  T  H  A  I  W  T  T  S  D  W  S  A  M  K
D  N  F  G  H  X  A  R  R  O  K  H  P  E  Q
P  Q  I  M  Z  L  I  D  E  T  J  A  Y  A  V
C  F  W  L  F  Q  W  U  F  B  U  R  D  X  F
T  F  E  B  R  E  I  T  E  G  L  P  O  V  E
S  S  A  B  G  A  L  M  R  T  V  E  V  F  L
L  I  R  W  B  A  B  U  U  S  T  R  K  Q  C
X  Y  X  R  R  N  Z  I  S  N  O  T  E  X  O
U  J  N  U  N  P  F  M  A  Q  T  J  K  Y  S
C  U  T  E  E  J  F  J  E  T  R  W  R  K  B
B  A  T  K  M  S  A  L  M  H  A  E  Q  J  X
N  K  F  O  C  V  T  X  F  H  J  E  S  W  G
S  X  K  Q  X  Q  S  S  V  N  V  S  B  T  W
A  C  C  E  N  T  I  U  X  J  W  O  Y  M  J
T  L  G  P  W  A  X  N  M  I  P  S  I  N  Z
```

ACCENT	MEASURE
BARLINE	NATURAL
BASS	NOTE
BEAT	REST
CLEF	SHARP
DOT	STAFF
FLAT	TIE
KEY	TREBLE

 Quiz 7 # Musical Terms in Italian

DIRECTIONS: Find the 12 words below in the grid. The words in the grid may be forward, backward, down, up, or diagonal. Each word will always be in a straight line. When you find the word, circle the letters.

```
A  Y  C  O  M  G  D  R  O  T  M  O  A  Z  R
O  S  J  D  B  U  A  S  E  N  T  A  D  Z  I
M  V  B  N  R  B  M  N  N  A  A  E  I  M  T
I  H  N  E  B  G  U  H  C  T  C  I  R  P  A
S  B  K  C  T  T  N  C  O  R  C  S  P  X  R
S  M  Y  S  O  O  A  F  E  R  M  A  T  A  D
I  F  U  E  K  T  M  S  P  X  Z  K  D  B  L
T  U  F  R  S  R  C  I  E  T  R  O  F  R  J
R  Q  A  C  U  E  L  M  S  D  Y  F  Q  I  J
O  A  H  T  N  L  C  P  A  S  G  I  W  D  N
F  N  K  D  U  G  D  W  Z  J  I  V  W  Y  S
M  B  O  A  Q  I  W  T  G  K  H  N  Z  O  X
R  J  Z  Y  V  O  T  A  C  R  A  M  A  H  V
J  A  C  C  E  L  E  R  A  N  D  O  C  I  P
P  H  S  X  G  X  L  H  M  G  U  P  Y  C  P
```

ACCELERANDO	MARCATO
CRESCENDO	PIANISSIMO
DECRESCENDO	PIANO
FERMATA	RITARD
FORTE	STACCATO
FORTISSIMO	TENUTO

Quiz 58

Musical Tempo Terms

Name: _____

Class: _____

DIRECTIONS: Find the 12 words below in the grid. The words in the grid may be forward, backward, down, up, or diagnonal. Each word will always be in a straight line. When you find the word, circle the letters.

```
V  O  E  D  G  S  A  W  A  C  Y  O  H  Q  V
J  L  D  S  R  O  V  L  S  V  D  S  C  N  E
M  O  D  E  R  A  T  O  L  N  B  L  T  A  N
X  A  A  I  X  Q  D  G  A  E  N  O  E  A  S
P  Z  J  Q  X  F  T  R  P  Q  G  W  L  N  E
A  F  B  T  O  I  E  N  A  W  T  R  J  D  C
C  O  X  L  G  L  A  A  Z  T  G  D  O  A  A
S  A  U  T  E  D  M  I  P  P  I  O  M  N  V
B  M  I  C  A  O  T  S  E  R  P  R  A  T  I
D  P  C  G  T  E  M  P  O  A  V  F  Y  E  V
Q  A  I  F  L  F  R  J  Y  C  D  X  O  Q  I
A  O  X  L  A  P  X  C  O  S  L  G  V  K  Y
O  I  M  O  Q  S  R  B  B  M  R  K  O  A  P
X  L  K  S  J  B  T  U  C  A  U  F  H  U  H
G  M  L  V  I  M  Z  V  L  W  O  A  J  K  Q
```

ACCELERANDO	MODERATO
ADAGIO	PRESTO
ALLEGRO	RITARD
ANDANTE	SLOW
FAST	TEMPO
LARGO	VIVACE

Name: _____

Class: _____

Quiz 59

Crossword: The Basics of Music

ACROSS

1. It divides two measures
6. Musical symbol which raises a note a half step
8. Not stop
9. What we do with food
10. Short for Sidney
11. Before noon
12. Musical symbol which lowers a note a half step
14. Treble and bass are this
15. The middle of a donut
17. Notes are in this on a staff
18. Note equal to two eighths
22. Abbr. for Nebraska
23. Santa's helper
24. One of five on your foot
27. Whole, half, quarter, and eighth are this
30. Note equal to two half notes
31. The notes and rests between two barlines; a unit of music

DOWN

1. The lowest male singing voice; also, a clef
2. What we do with a book
3. Note equal to one half of a quarter
4. Type of clef, not the bass
5. Notes are on this…lines and spaces
7. Hello
13. Notes are on this on a staff
14. Not dirty
16. Note equal to two quarters
17. To look
19. Silence in music
20. Short for Edward
21. Not one
25. To heal
26. Placed after a note, it means to add half to note's value
28. Hello in Spanish
29. Australian bird that can't fly
30. Us

Name: _____

Class: _____

Quiz 60

Crossword: Musical Terms

ACROSS

1. Musical term for soft
3. Abbr. for United States of America
6. After noon
9. Sick
10. Gradually increase in volume
11. Italian musical term meaning very slow tempo
12. To wager
13. Short for Ronald
14. Line above or below a note meaning to hold a note for its full value
15. Dynamite!
17. Short for Susan
18. One plus one
19. Abbr. for cresecendo
22. Musical symbol indicating that a note should be held for more than its normal value
25. Abbr. for Virginia
26. Musical term meaning loud
27. Abbr. for Pennsylvania
28. Musical term meaning to slow the tempo
30. Roman garment
31. Abbreviation for Oregon
32. Not dry
33. Abbr. for mister
37. Abbr. for Tennessee
38. Musical term meaning medium: _____ forte
39. In a moderate tempo

DOWN

1. Politically correct, or personal computer
2. Musical symbol meaning to emphasize a note
4. Italian musical term meaning a cheerful or fast tempo
5. Italian musical term meaning a moderate, graceful tempo
7. Musical symbol meaning to strongly emphasize a note
8. Gradually decrease in volume
10. Corn on the _____
11. Short for Leonard
16. Trick or _____
18. Curved line above or below two notes that combines the duration of the note values
20. Abbr. for San Francisco
21. Italian musical term meaning a very slow tempo
23. Not before
24. Also
25. Italian musical term meaning a lively, quick tempo
27. Italian musical term meaning a very fast tempo
29. Abbr. for Alaska
33. Mother
34. Abbr. for American Automobile Association
35. A wizard came from here
36. Abbr. for Delaware

ANSWERS

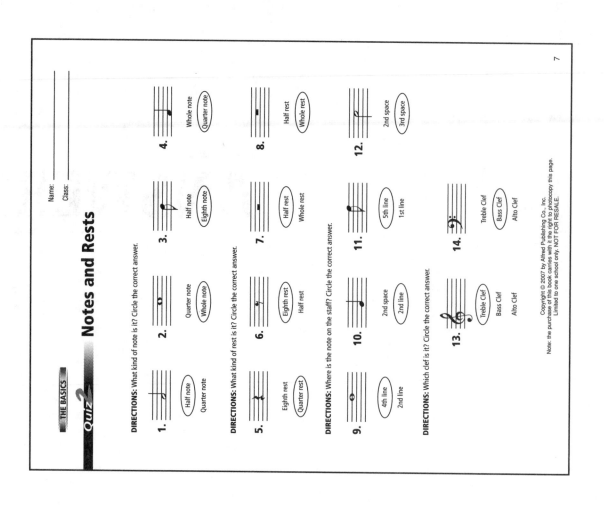

THE BASICS

Quiz 2 — Notes and Rests

Name: _____
Class: _____

DIRECTIONS: What kind of note is it? Circle the correct answer.

1. Half note / Quarter note
2. Quarter note / Whole note
3. Half note / Eighth note
4. Whole note / Quarter note

DIRECTIONS: What kind of rest is it? Circle the correct answer.

5. Eighth rest / Quarter rest
6. Eighth rest / Half rest
7. Half rest / Whole rest
8. Half rest / Whole rest

DIRECTIONS: Where is the note on the staff? Circle the correct answer.

9. 4th line / 2nd line
10. 2nd space / 2nd line
11. 5th line / 1st line
12. 2nd space / 3rd space

DIRECTIONS: Which clef is it? Circle the correct answer.

13. Treble Clef / Bass Clef / Alto Clef
14. Treble Clef / Bass Clef / Alto Clef

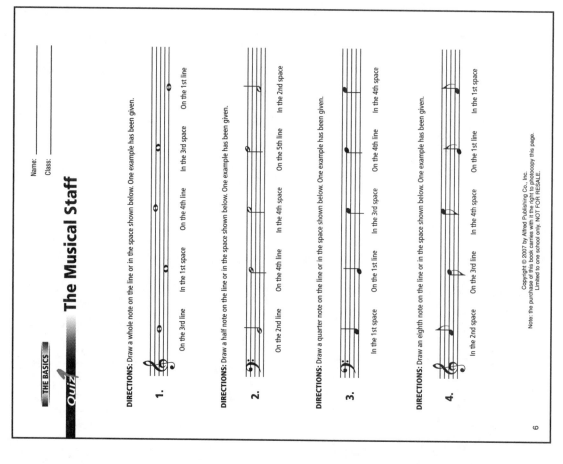

THE BASICS

Quiz 1 — The Musical Staff

Name: _____
Class: _____

DIRECTIONS: Draw a whole note on the line or in the space shown below. One example has been given.

1. On the 3rd line / In the 1st space / On the 4th line / In the 3rd space / On the 1st line

DIRECTIONS: Draw a half note on the line or in the space shown below. One example has been given.

2. On the 2nd line / On the 4th line / In the 4th space / On the 5th line / In the 2nd space

DIRECTIONS: Draw a quarter note on the line or in the space shown below. One example has been given.

3. In the 1st space / On the 1st line / In the 3rd space / On the 4th line / In the 4th space

DIRECTIONS: Draw an eighth note on the line or in the space shown below. One example has been given.

4. In the 2nd space / On the 3rd line / In the 4th space / On the 1st line / In the 1st space

THE BASICS

Quiz 4 — Note Values

Name: _____
Class: _____

DIRECTIONS: True or false? Circle the correct answer for each example.

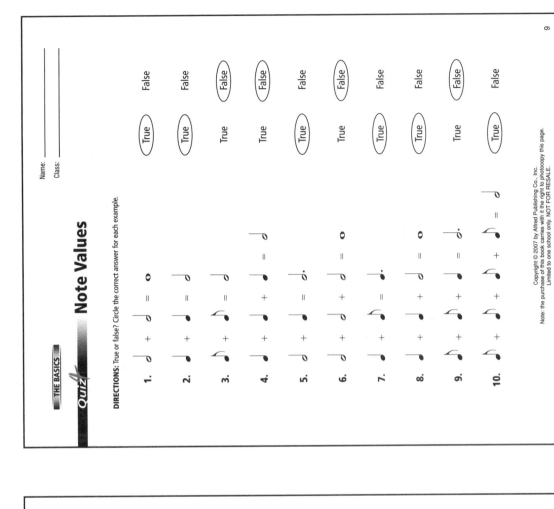

1. 𝅗𝅥 + 𝅗𝅥 = 𝅝   (True)   False

2. ♩ + 𝅗𝅥 = 𝅗𝅥   (True)   False

3. ♪ + ♩ = 𝅗𝅥   True   False

4. ♩ + ♩ = 𝅗𝅥   True   False

5. 𝅗𝅥 + ♩ = 𝅗𝅥.   (True)   False

6. 𝅗𝅥 + 𝅗𝅥 = 𝅝   True   False

7. ♩ + ♩ = ♩.   (True)   False

8. 𝅗𝅥 + ♩ = 𝅝   (True)   False

9. ♪ + ♩ = 𝅗𝅥.   True   False

10. ♪ + ♩ = 𝅗𝅥   (True)   False

THE BASICS

Quiz 3 — Know Your Notes and Rests

Name: _____
Class: _____

DIRECTIONS: Name each note or rest. Write the correct letter from the second column in the blank space.

1. _E_

2. _A_

3. _H_

4. _B_

5. _C_

6. _G_

7. _F_

8. _D_

A. Eighth Note

B. Eighth Rest

C. Quarter Note

D. Quarter Rest

E. Half Note

F. Half Rest

G. Whole Note

H. Whole Rest

DIRECTIONS: The arrow points to a part of a note. Name that part of the note. Write the correct letter from the second column in the blank space.

9. _K_

10. _I_

11. _L_

12. _J_

I. Stem

J. Beam

K. Notehead

L. Flag

Name: _____

Class: _____

Quiz — Note and Rest Values

DIRECTIONS: True or false? Are the number of beats in the first example equal to the number of beats in the second example? Circle the correct answer.

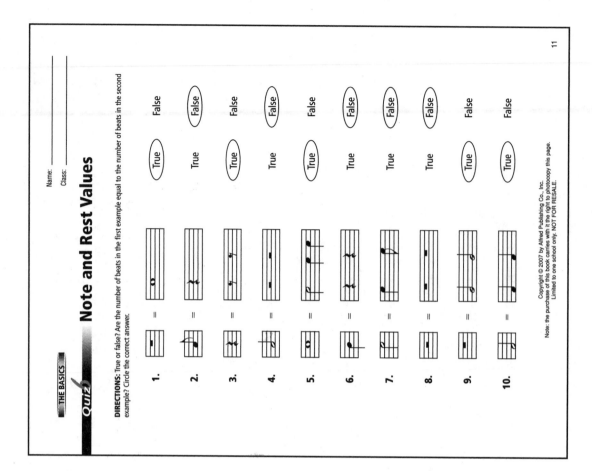

1. True   False
2. True   False
3. True   False
4. True   False
5. True   False
6. True   False
7. True   False
8. True   False
9. True   False
10. True   False

Name: _____

Class: _____

Quiz — Rest Values

DIRECTIONS: True or false? Circle the correct answer for each example.

1. True   False
2. True   False
3. True   False
4. True   False
5. True   False
6. True   False
7. True   False
8. True   False
9. True   False
10. True   False

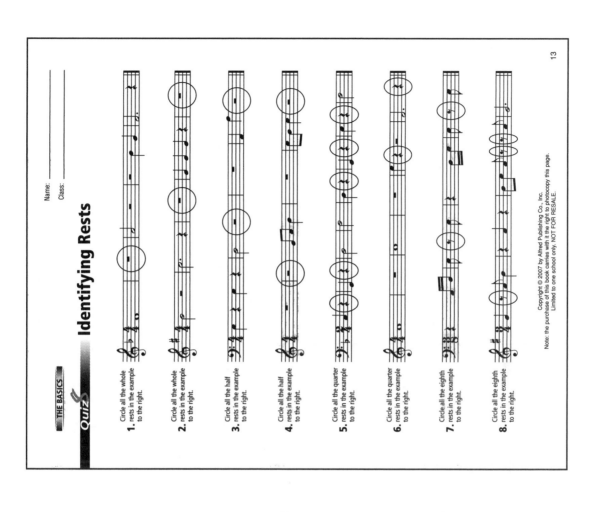

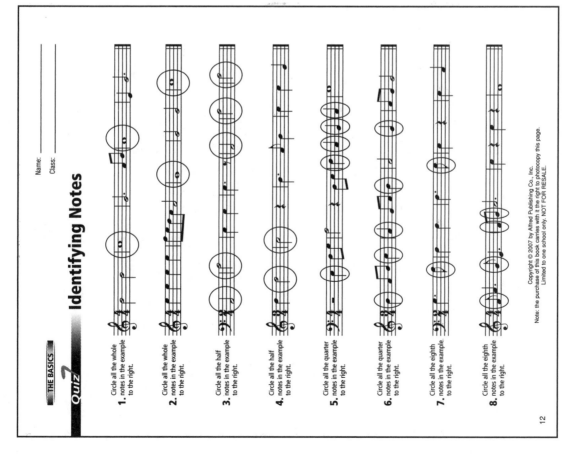

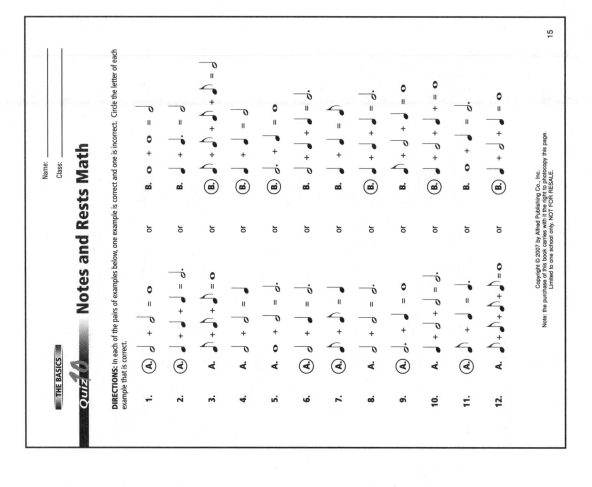

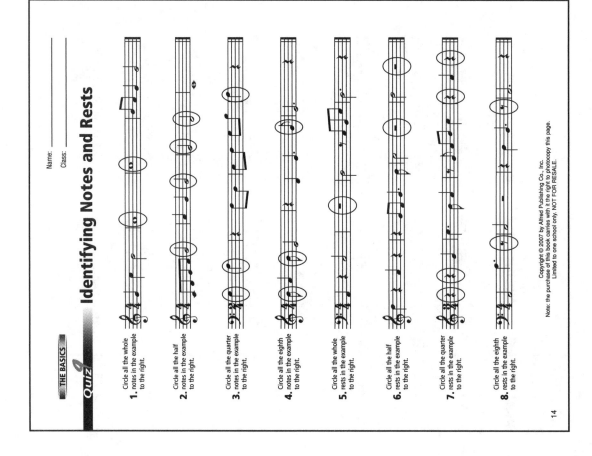

Quiz 11 Do You Know Your Notes and Rests?

Name: _____

Class: _____

DIRECTIONS: The left example has one note in the staff. In the blank staff to the right, draw two notes which equal the note in the left example.

1. [staff] =

2. [staff] =

3. [staff] =

6. [staff] =

DIRECTIONS: The left example has one rest in the staff. In the blank staff to the right, draw two rests which equal the rest in the left example.

4. [staff] =

5. [staff] =

DIRECTIONS: The left example has one note in the staff. In the blank staff to the right, draw four notes which equal the note in the left example.

7. [staff] =

8. [staff] =

DIRECTIONS: The left example has one rest in the staff. In the blank staff to the right, draw four rests which equal the rest in the left example.

9. [staff] =

10. [staff] =

16

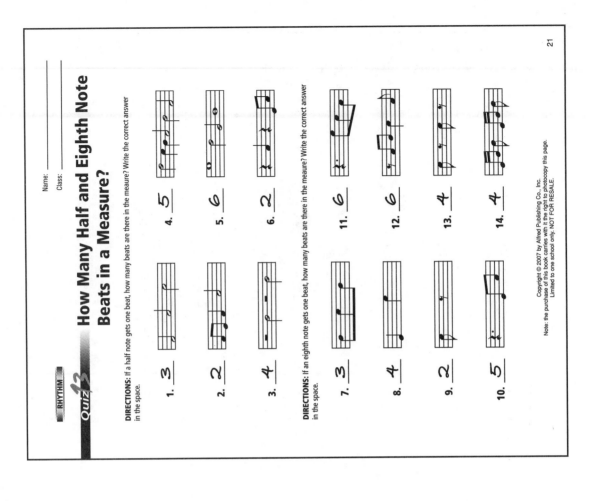

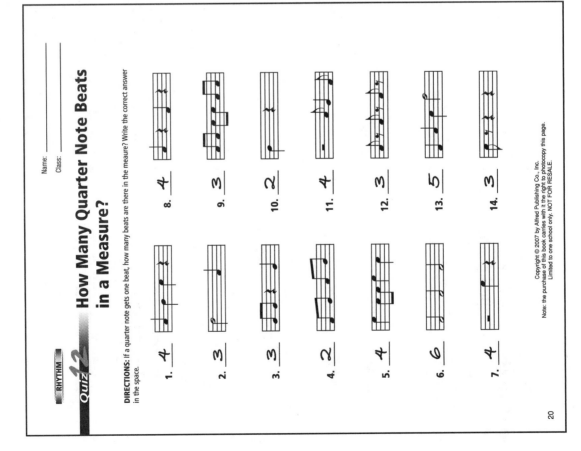

Quiz 15

Barlines and Measures—
Half and Eighth Note Beat

Name: _____
Class: _____

DIRECTIONS: In examples 1–4 below, a half note gets one beat.

In examples 1 and 2, draw barlines after every three beats.

1.

2.

In examples 3 and 4, draw barlines after every two beats.

3.

4.

DIRECTIONS: In examples 5–8 below, an eighth note gets one beat.

In examples 5 and 6, draw barlines after every six beats.

5.

6.

In example 7, draw barlines after every four beats.

7.

In example 8, draw barlines after every three beats.

8.

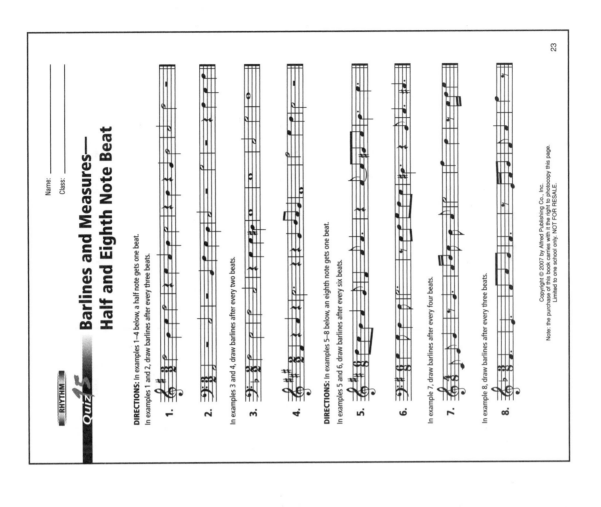

Quiz 14

Barlines and Measures—
Quarter Note Beat

Name: _____
Class: _____

DIRECTIONS: In the examples below, a quarter note gets one beat.

In examples 1, 2, and 3, draw barlines after every four beats.

1.

2.

3.

In examples 4, 5, and 6, draw barlines after every three beats.

4.

5.

6.

In examples 7 and 8, draw barlines after every two beats.

7.

8.

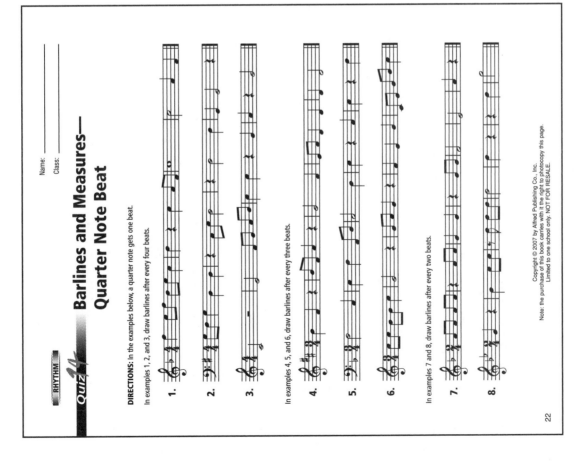

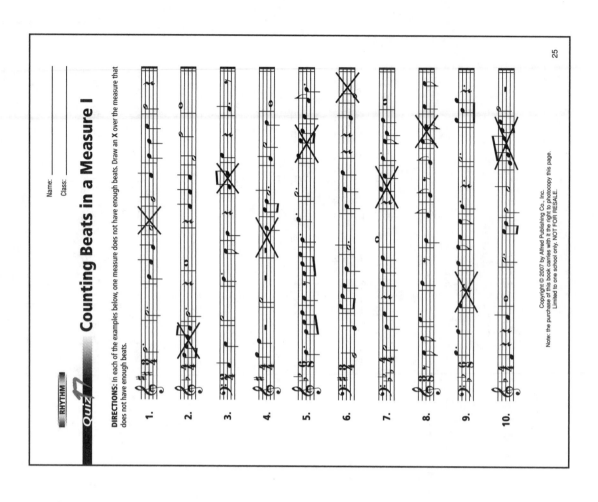

Quiz 17 — Counting Beats in a Measure I

Name: _____
Class: _____

DIRECTIONS: In each of the examples below, one measure does not have enough beats. Draw an **X** over the measure that does not have enough beats.

1.
2.
3.
4.
5.
6.
7.
8.
9.
10.

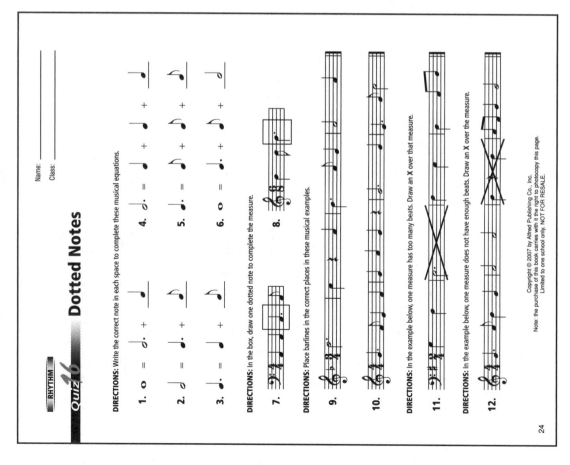

Quiz 16 — Dotted Notes

Name: _____
Class: _____

DIRECTIONS: Write the correct note in each space to complete these musical equations.

1. 𝅝 = 𝅗𝅥. + ___
2. 𝅗𝅥 = 𝅘𝅥. + ___
3. 𝅘𝅥. = 𝅘𝅥 + ___

4. 𝅗𝅥. = ___ + ___
5. ___ = ___ + ___
6. 𝅝 = ___ + ___ + ___

DIRECTIONS: In the box, draw one dotted note to complete the measure.

7.
8.

DIRECTIONS: Place barlines in the correct places in these musical examples.

9.
10.

DIRECTIONS: In the example below, one measure has too many beats. Draw an **X** over that measure.

11.

DIRECTIONS: In the example below, one measure does not have enough beats. Draw an **X** over the measure.

12.

RHYTHM
Quiz 19   Add the Missing Note

Name: _____
Class: _____

DIRECTIONS: One note is missing in each measure. Write one note in each box to complete the measure. Put the note on any line or in any space. (Remember, the time signature will tell you how many beats are in each measure, and what note gets a beat.)

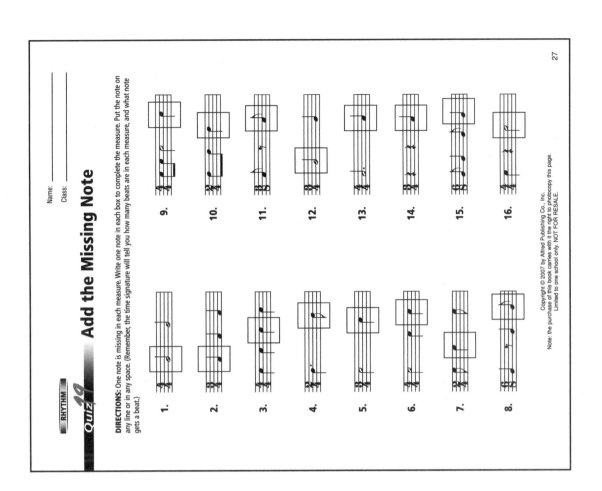

RHYTHM
Quiz 18   Counting Beats in a Measure II

Name: _____
Class: _____

DIRECTIONS: In each of the examples below, one measure has too many beats. Draw an **X** over the measure that has too many beats.

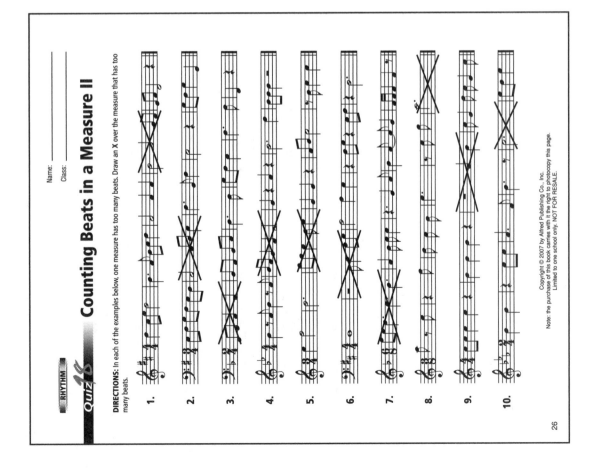

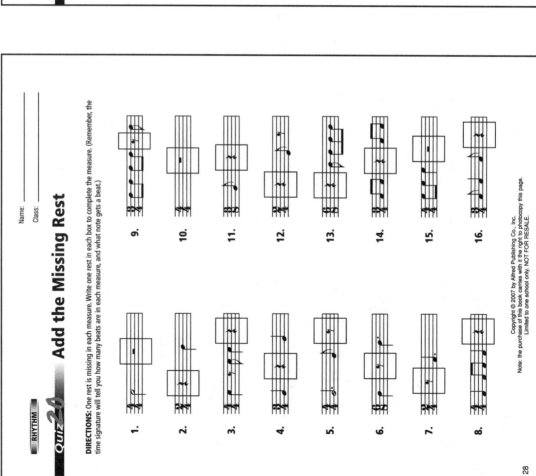

RHYTHM

Quiz 21 — Tied Notes

Name: _____
Class: _____

DIRECTIONS: To figure out the value of the two tied notes, add the value of both notes. Are the following musical examples correct? Circle True or False.

1. (True) False
2. (False) True
3. (True) False
4. (True) False
5. (True) False
6. (True) False
7. (True) False
8. (True) False

DIRECTIONS: In the blank space, draw the note or dotted note that equals the two tied notes.

9.
10.
11.
12.

DIRECTIONS: In the blank space, draw the correct note or dotted note to the tied note to complete the musical equation.

13.
14.
15.
16.

RHYTHM

Quiz 20 — Add the Missing Rest

Name: _____
Class: _____

DIRECTIONS: One rest is missing in each measure. Write one rest in each box to complete the measure. (Remember, the time signature will tell you how many beats are in each measure, and what note gets a beat.)

1.
2.
3.
4.
5.
6.
7.
8.
9.
10.
11.
12.
13.
14.
15.
16.

Quiz 22 — Musical Equations

Name: _____

Class: _____

DIRECTIONS: These questions will test your knowledge of note values. Write a number in the blank which completes the musical equation.

1. ♪ × __2__ = ♩
2. ♪ × __4__ = 𝅗𝅥
3. 𝅗𝅥 × __2__ = 𝅝
4. ♬ × __8__ = 𝅝
5. ♩ × __4__ = 𝅝
6. ♬ × __4__ = ♩
7. ♩ × __2__ = 𝅗𝅥
8. ♪ × __8__ = 𝅝

DIRECTIONS: In the blanks space below, draw one note equal to the value of the notes in the musical equation. You may use dotted notes.

9. ♩ + ♩ = _____
10. ♪ + ♪ + ♪ + ♪ = _____
11. ♬ + ♩ = _____
12. ♩ + ♪ + ♪ = _____
13. ♬ + ♩ + ♩ = _____
14. ♬ + ♬ = _____
15. ♩ + ♩ + ♩ = _____
16. 𝅗𝅥 + ♩ + ♩ = _____
17. ♪ + ♪ + ♪ + ♩ = _____
18. ♬ + ♩ = _____
19. ♩. + ♩ = _____
20. ♬ + ♩ + ♩ = _____
21. ♩ + 𝅗𝅥 = _____
22. ♩ + ♩ + ♩ = _____
23. ♩ + ♩ = _____
24. ♪ + ♩ = _____

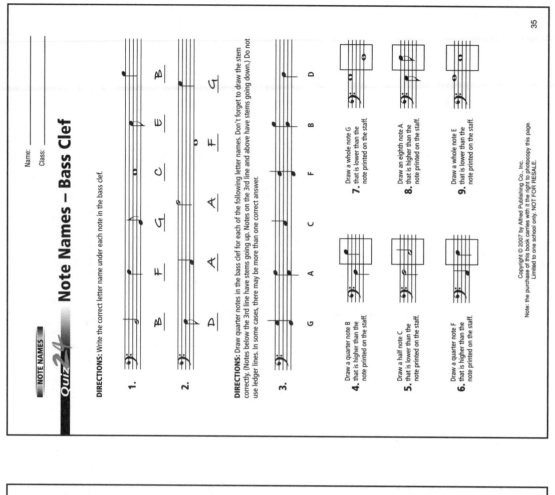

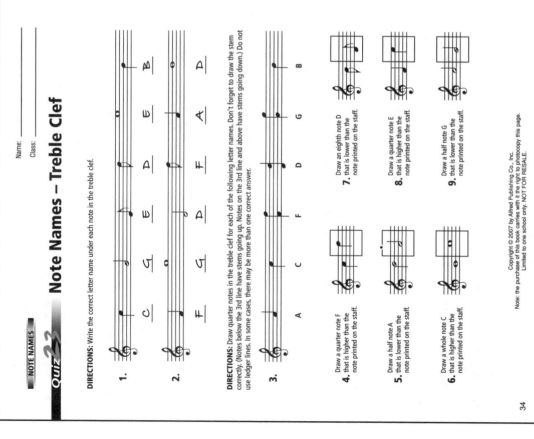

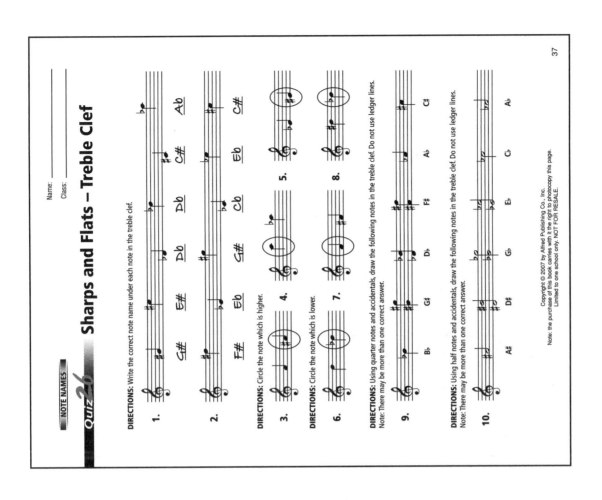

NOTE NAMES

QUIZ 26 — Sharps and Flats – Treble Clef

Name: _____
Class: _____

DIRECTIONS: Write the correct note name under each note in the treble clef.

1. G♯   E♯   D♭   D♭   C♯   A♭

2. _____   E♭   G♭   C♭   E♭   C♯

DIRECTIONS: Circle the note which is higher. 3.   4.

DIRECTIONS: Circle the note which is lower. 6.   7.

5.   8.

DIRECTIONS: Using quarter notes and accidentals, draw the following notes in the treble clef. Do not use ledger lines. Note: There may be more than one correct answer.

9.   B♭   G♯   D♭   F♯   A♭   C♯

DIRECTIONS: Using half notes and accidentals, draw the following notes in the treble clef. Do not use ledger lines. Note: There may be more than one correct answer.

10.   A♯   D♯   E♭   G♭   C♭   A♭

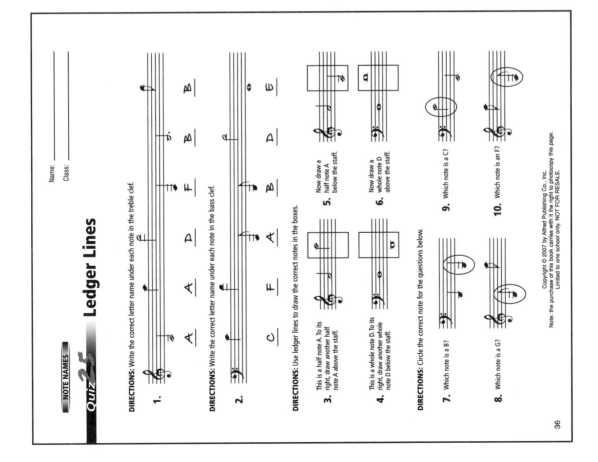

NOTE NAMES

QUIZ 25 — Ledger Lines

Name: _____
Class: _____

DIRECTIONS: Write the correct letter name under each note in the treble clef.

1.   A   A   D   F   B   B

DIRECTIONS: Write the correct letter name under each note in the bass clef.

2.   C   F   A   B   D   E

DIRECTIONS: Use ledger lines to draw the correct notes in the boxes.

3. This is a half note A. To its right, draw another half note A above the staff.

4. This is a whole note D. To its right, draw another whole note D below the staff.

5. Now draw a half note A below the staff.

6. Now draw a whole note D above the staff.

DIRECTIONS: Circle the correct note for the questions below.

7. Which note is a B?

8. Which note is a G?

9. Which note is a C?

10. Which note is an F?

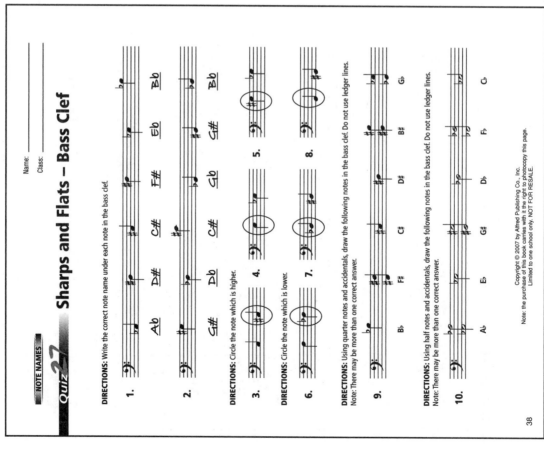

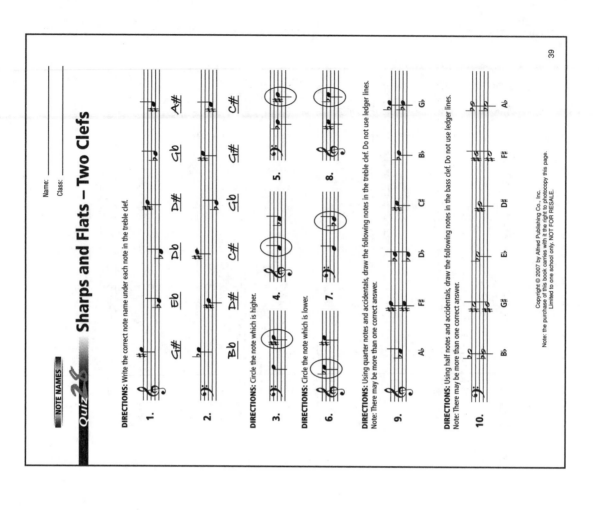

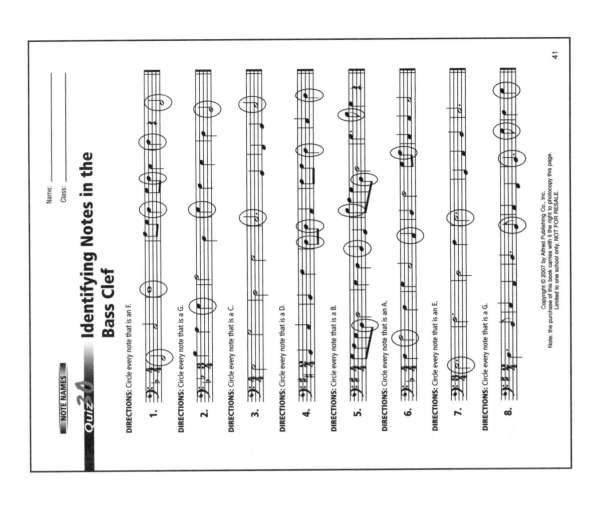

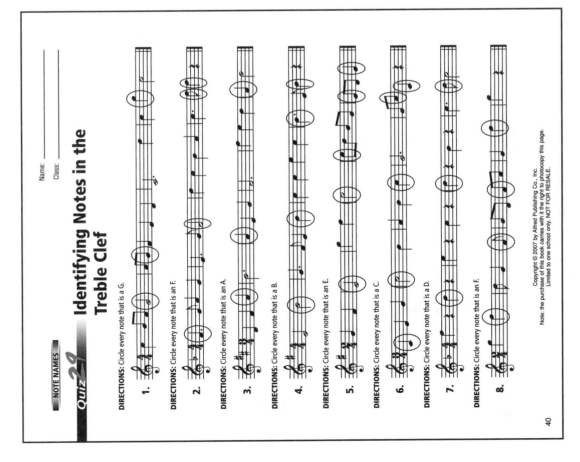

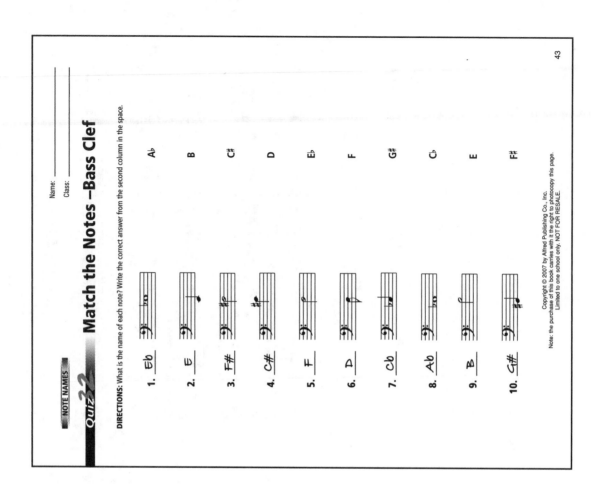

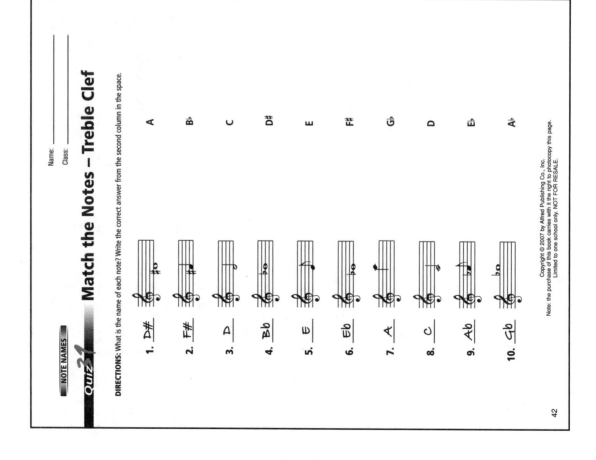

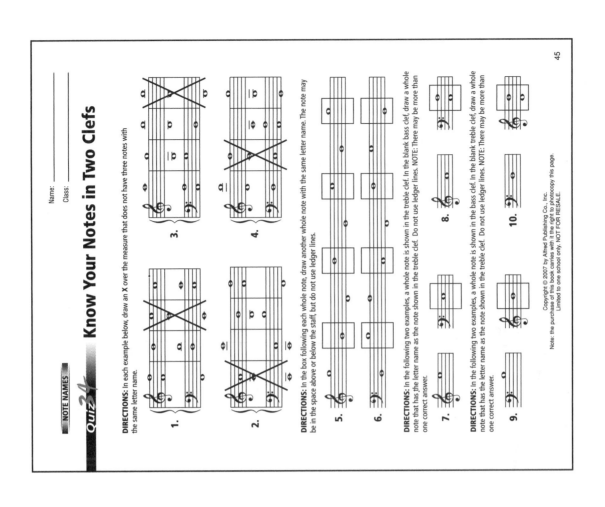

QUIZ 34 Know Your Notes in Two Clefs

Name: _____

Class: _____

DIRECTIONS: In each example below, draw an X over the measure that does not have three notes with the same letter name.

1.

2.

3.

4.

DIRECTIONS: In the box following each whole note, draw another whole note with the same letter name. The note may be in the space above or below the staff, but do not use ledger lines.

5.

6.

DIRECTIONS: In the following two examples, a whole note is shown in the treble clef. In the blank bass clef, draw a whole note that has the same letter name as the note shown in the treble clef. Do not use ledger lines. NOTE: There may be more than one correct answer.

7.

8.

DIRECTIONS: In the following two examples, a whole note is shown in the treble clef. In the blank treble clef, draw a whole note that has the same letter name as the note shown in the bass clef. Do not use ledger lines. NOTE: There may be more than one correct answer.

9.

10.

QUIZ 33 Note Names – Treble and Bass Clef

Name: _____

Class: _____

DIRECTIONS: Draw an X over any note that is not an F.

1.

DIRECTIONS: Directions: Draw an X over any note that is not an A.

2.

DIRECTIONS: Directions: Draw an X over any note that is not an E.

3.

DIRECTIONS: Directions: Draw an X over any note that is not a D.

4.

DIRECTIONS: In the following examples, draw an X over the measure that does not have two notes with the same letter name.

5.

6.

DIRECTIONS: True or False? Are the notes the same? Circle T or F.

7. = (T) F

8. = T (F)

9. = (T) F

10. = T (F)

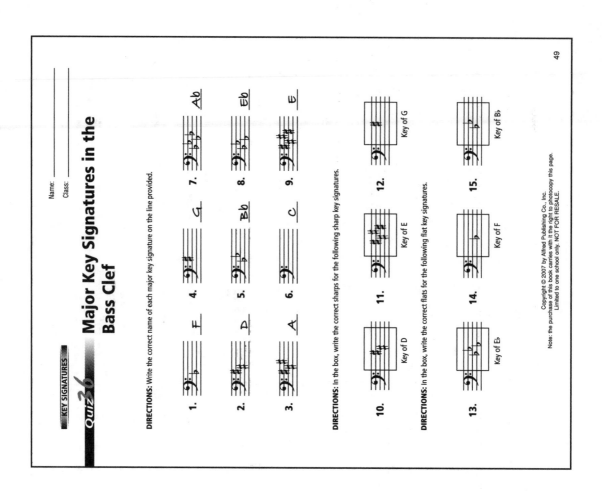

Quiz 36 · Major Key Signatures in the Bass Clef

Name: _____
Class: _____

DIRECTIONS: Write the correct name of each major key signature on the line provided.

1. F   4. G   7. Ab
2. D   5. Bb   8. Eb
3. A   6. C   9. E

DIRECTIONS: In the box, write the correct sharps for the following sharp key signatures.

10. Key of D   11. Key of E   12. Key of G

DIRECTIONS: In the box, write the correct flats for the following flat key signatures.

13. Key of Eb   14. Key of F   15. Key of Bb

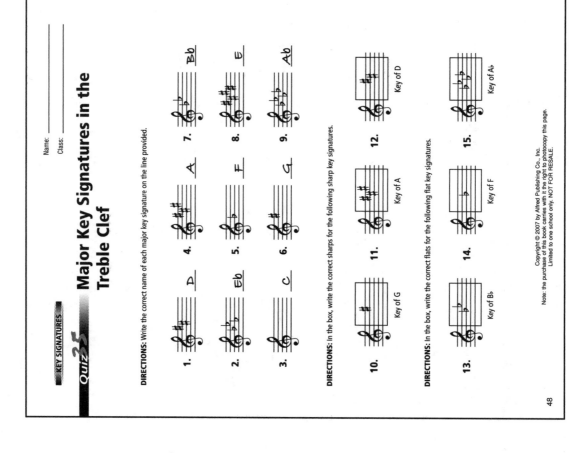

Quiz 35 · Major Key Signatures in the Treble Clef

Name: _____
Class: _____

DIRECTIONS: Write the correct name of each major key signature on the line provided.

1. D   4. A   7. Bb
2. Eb   5. F   8. E
3. C   6. G   9. Ab

DIRECTIONS: In the box, write the correct sharps for the following sharp key signatures.

10. Key of G   11. Key of A   12. Key of D

DIRECTIONS: In the box, write the correct flats for the following flat key signatures.

13. Key of Bb 14. Key of F   15. Key of Ab

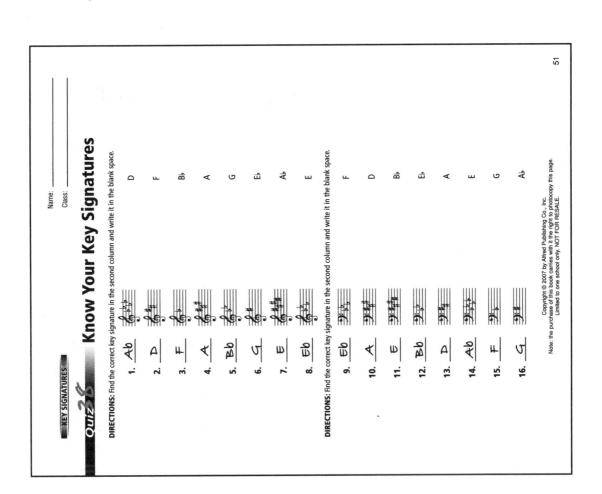

KEY SIGNATURES

Quiz 38 Know Your Key Signatures

Name: _____
Class: _____

DIRECTIONS: Find the correct key signature in the second column and write it in the blank space.

1. Ab — D
2. D — F
3. F — Bb
4. A — A
5. Bb — G
6. G — Eb
7. E — Ab
8. Eb — E

DIRECTIONS: Find the correct key signature in the second column and write it in the blank space.

9. Eb — F
10. A — D
11. E — Bb
12. Bb — Eb
13. D — A
14. Ab — E
15. F — G
16. G — Ab

51

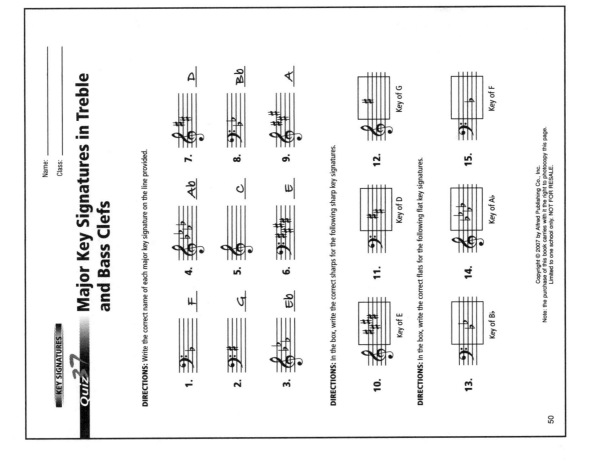

KEY SIGNATURES

Quiz 37 Major Key Signatures in Treble and Bass Clefs

Name: _____
Class: _____

DIRECTIONS: Write the correct name of each major key signature on the line provided.

1. F
2. G
3. Eb
4. Ab
5. C
6. E
7. D
8. Bb
9. A

DIRECTIONS: In the box, write the correct sharps for the following sharp key signatures.

10. Key of E
11. Key of D
12. Key of G

DIRECTIONS: In the box, write the correct flats for the following flat key signatures.

13. Key of Bb
14. Key of Ab
15. Key of F

50

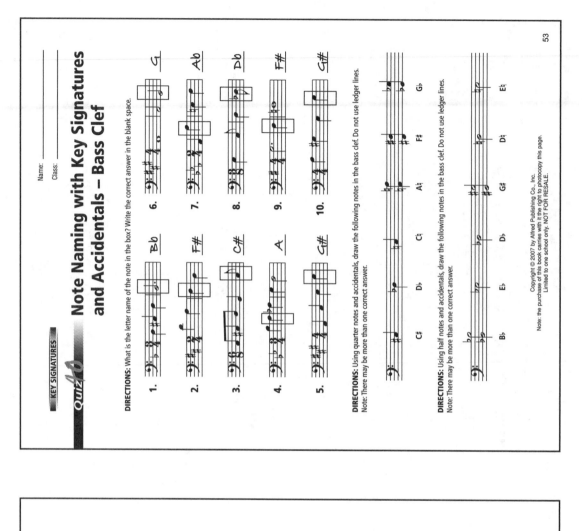

Name: _____

Class: _____

Quiz A Accidentals in Treble and Bass Clefs

DIRECTIONS: What is the letter name of the note in the box? Write the correct answer in the blank space.

1. B♭
2. C♮
3. C#
4. B♭
5. C♮
6. E♭
7. E♭
8. D#
9. F#
10. B♭

DIRECTIONS: Using half notes and accidentals, draw the following notes in the treble clef. Do not use ledger lines.
Note: There may be more than one correct answer.

A♭   G#   B♮   C#   F♮   D♭

DIRECTIONS: Using whole notes and accidentals, draw the following notes in the bass clef. Do not use ledger lines.
Note: There may be more than one correct answer.

E♮   C♭   D#   F#   B♭   G#

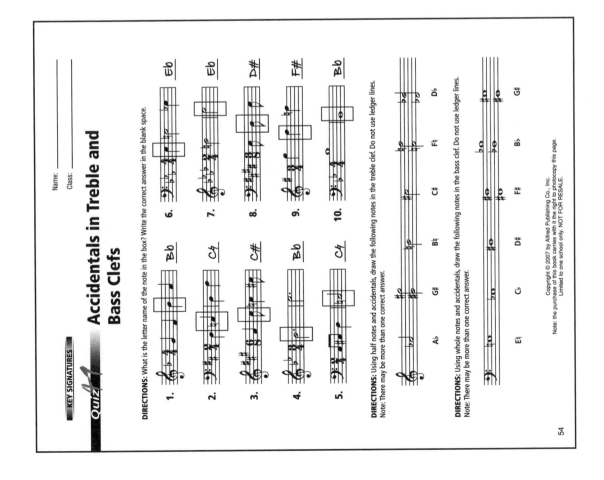

54

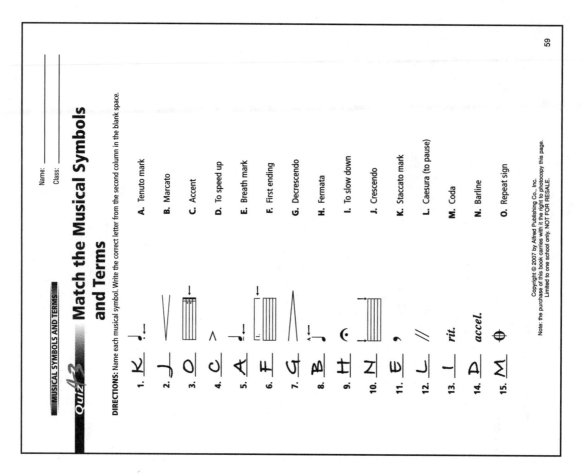

Quiz A2 Match the Musical Symbols and Terms

Name: _____
Class: _____

DIRECTIONS: Name each musical symbol. Write the correct letter from the second column in the blank space.

1. K
2. J
3. O
4. C
5. A
6. F
7. G
8. B
9. H
10. N
11. E
12. L
13. I
14. D
15. M

A. Tenuto mark
B. Marcato
C. Accent
D. To speed up
E. Breath mark
F. First ending
G. Decrescendo
H. Fermata
I. To slow down
J. Crescendo
K. Staccato mark
L. Caesura (to pause)
M. Coda
N. Barline
O. Repeat sign

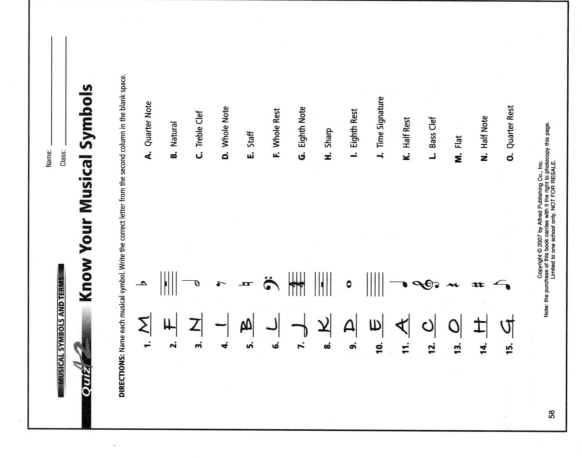

Quiz A2 Know Your Musical Symbols

Name: _____
Class: _____

DIRECTIONS: Name each musical symbol. Write the correct letter from the second column in the blank space.

1. M
2. F
3. N
4. I
5. B
6. L
7. J
8. K
9. D
10. E
11. A
12. C
13. O
14. H
15. G

A. Quarter Note
B. Natural
C. Treble Clef
D. Whole Note
E. Staff
F. Whole Rest
G. Eighth Note
H. Sharp
I. Eighth Rest
J. Time Signature
K. Half Rest
L. Bass Clef
M. Flat
N. Half Note
O. Quarter Rest

Quiz 44 Which Is It? Musical Symbols

Name: _____
Class: _____

DIRECTIONS: Which is it? Circle the letter of the correct answer for each example.

1. This is a — (A.) Time Signature — B. Key Signature
2. This is a — (A.) Whole Rest — B. Half Rest
3. This is a — A. Half Note — (B.) Whole Note
4. These are — A. Quarter Notes — (B.) Eighth Notes
5. This is a — (A.) Fermata — B. Tie
6. This is a — A. Sharp — (B.) Flat
7. This is a — (A.) Bass clef sign — B. Treble clef sign
8. This is a — A. Natural — (B.) Sharp
9. This is a — A. Half Rest — (B.) Quarter Rest
10. This means — A. Loud — (B.) Soft
11. This means — A. Get faster — (B.) Get slower
12. This means — (A.) Get louder — B. Get softer
13. This is an — A. Eighth Rest — (B.) Accent
14. This means — A. Stop playing — (B.) Repeat the section
15. This dot means — (A.) The note is short — B. The note is long

---

Quiz 45 How Loud? How Soft? Dynamics

Name: _____
Class: _____

DIRECTIONS: Which dynamic level is louder? Circle the correct answer.

1. p or (mp)   3. (f) or p
2. ff or (ff)   4. (mf) or mp

DIRECTIONS: Which dynamic level is softer? Circle the correct answer.

5. (p) or f 7. ff or (f)
6. (mp) or mf 8. f or (mp)

DIRECTIONS: What does each dynamic level mean? Write the correct letter from the second column in the blank space.

9. __F__ p A. Loud
10. __C__ mf B. Very soft
11. __E__ ff C. Medium loud
12. __D__ mp D. Medium soft
13. __A__ f E. Very loud
14. __B__ pp F. Soft

DIRECTIONS: Match the Italian term with each dynamic level. Write the correct letter from the second column in the blank space.

15. __B__ p A. *pianissimo*
16. __D__ mf B. *piano*
17. __F__ ff C. *mezzo piano*
18. __C__ mp D. *mezzo forte*
19. __E__ f E. *forte*
20. __A__ pp F. *fortissimo*

Quiz 17 How Fast? How Slow? Tempo

Name: _____
Class: _____

DIRECTIONS: Which tempo marking is faster? Circle the correct answer.

1. Largo   or   (Presto)
2. Moderato   or   (Vivace)
3. (Vivace)   or   Adagio
4. Andante   or   (Allegro)

DIRECTIONS: Which tempo marking is slower? Circle the correct answer.

5. Presto   or   (Andante)
6. (Adagio)   or   Presto
7. (Moderato)   or   Vivace
8. Andante   or   (Largo)

DIRECTIONS: What does each tempo marking mean? Write the correct letter from the second column in the blank space.

9. __A__ Allegro   A. Fast
10. __E__ Vivace   B. Very slow
11. __C__ Andante   C. Walking tempo
12. __B__ Largo   D. A moderate speed
13. __D__ Moderato   E. Very fast
14. __F__ Adagio   F. Slow

DIRECTIONS: What does each tempo change mean? Write the correct letter from the second column in the blank space.

15. __A__ ritardando   A. gradually slower
16. __B__ accelerando   B. gradually faster
17. __C__ a tempo   C. return to previous tempo

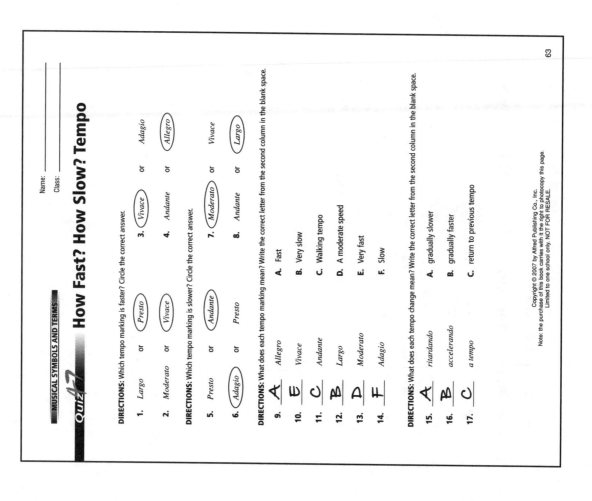

Quiz 16 Know Your Musical Dynamics

Name: _____
Class: _____

DIRECTIONS: Write the letter of the correct answer in the blank space.

1. _Decrescendo_ means the same as __A__

   A. Diminuendo
   B. Crescendo

2. ⟋ means A

   A. to gradually get louder
   B. to gradually get softer

DIRECTIONS: In the examples below, are the dynamics correct or incorrect? Circle the correct answer.

1. Correct   or   (Incorrect)
2. (Correct)   or   Incorrect
3. (Correct)   or   Incorrect
4. Correct   or   (Incorrect)

DIRECTIONS: How loud or soft is the music at Ⓐ, Ⓑ, Ⓒ and Ⓓ? Circle the correct answer.

5.
Ⓐ (Soft)   or   Loud   or   Very soft
Ⓑ (Medium loud)   or   Medium Soft   or   Very loud
Ⓒ Medium soft   or   Very Soft

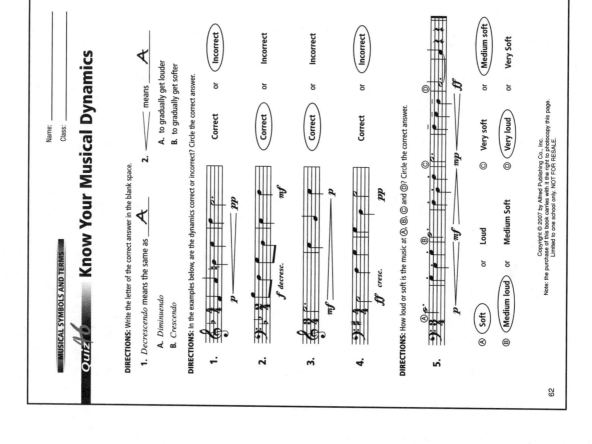

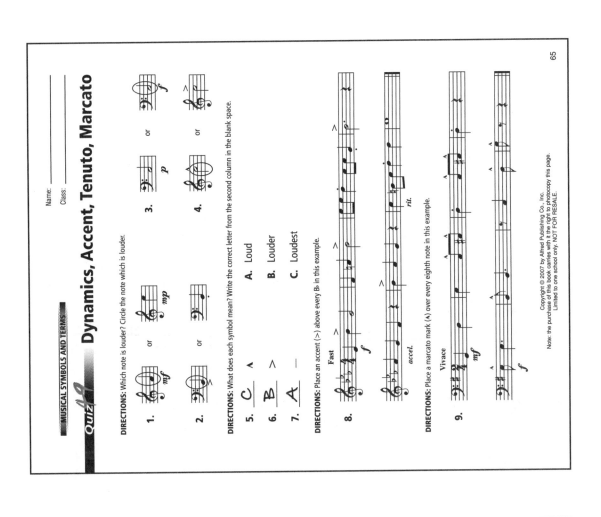

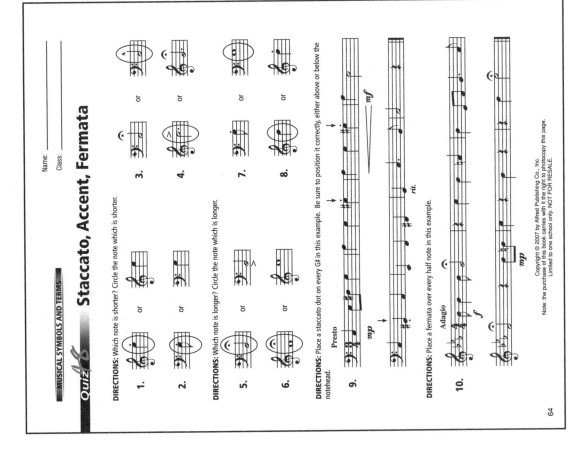

TIME SIGNATURES

Quiz 51 More Time Signatures: $\frac{2}{4}$, $\frac{3}{4}$, $\frac{4}{4}$

DIRECTIONS: Write the correct time signature in the box. The answer will be $\frac{2}{4}$, $\frac{3}{4}$, or $\frac{4}{4}$.

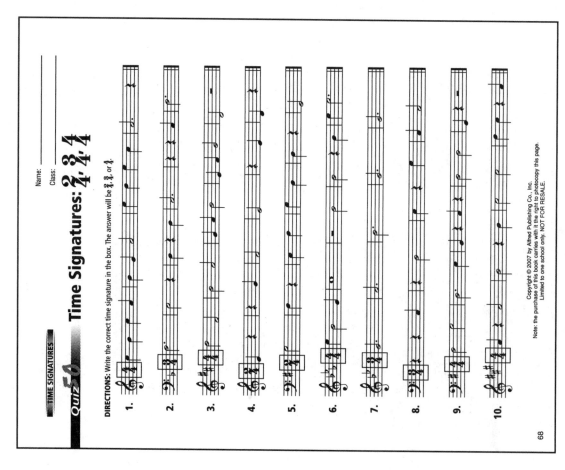

TIME SIGNATURES

Quiz 50 Time Signatures: $\frac{2}{4}$, $\frac{3}{4}$, $\frac{4}{4}$

DIRECTIONS: Write the correct time signature in the box. The answer will be $\frac{2}{4}$, $\frac{3}{4}$, or $\frac{4}{4}$.

Quiz 52 Advanced Time Signatures

Name: _____

Class: _____

DIRECTIONS: Write the correct time signature in the box. The answer will be $\frac{5}{4}$, $\frac{6}{4}$, $\frac{8}{4}$, $\frac{5}{8}$, or $\frac{6}{8}$.

113

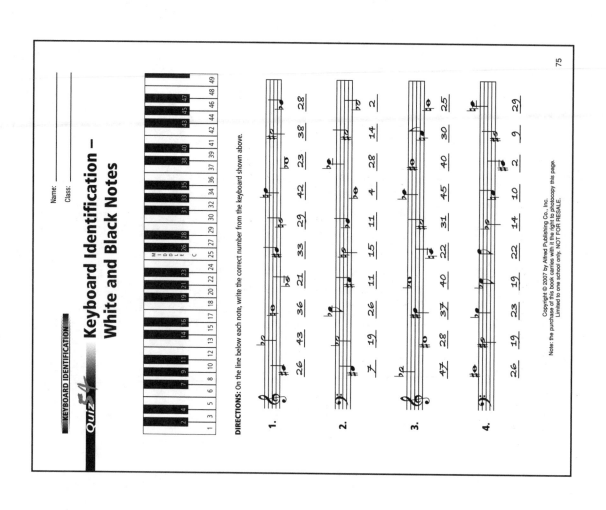

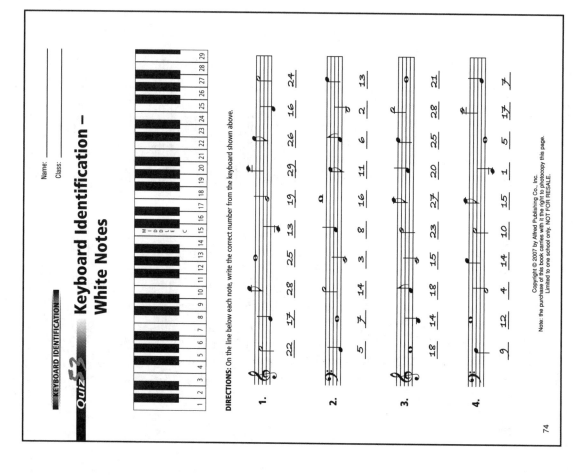

Quiz 55 — Unscramble the Musical Terms

Name: _____
Class: _____

DIRECTIONS: The left column contains musical terms. Unscramble the words in the right column. The right column contains scrambled words. Unscramble the words in the right column and match them with the musical terms in the left column. Place the correct letter from the right column in the blank space.

1. **M** accent
2. **C** pianissimo
3. **Q** flat
4. **G** tie
5. **N** piano
6. **L** forte
7. **S** marcato
8. **I** tempo
9. **H** clef
10. **K** natural
11. **A** staff
12. **T** tenuto
13. **O** fortissimo
14. **R** crescendo
15. **B** barline
16. **E** fermata
17. **F** decrescendo
18. **P** staccato
19. **J** measure
20. **D** sharp

A. ftafs
B. labenir
C. spsaiminio
D. parhs
E. meartfa
F. rsdceceoedn
G. eti
H. felc
I. poemt
J. sremuea
K. alnutra
L. rofet
M. ceatcn
N. anoip
O. sifromotsi
P. acsotatc
Q. falt
R. eodescrm
S. taormca
T. utneot

Quiz 56 — Musical Terms in English

Name: _____
Class: _____

DIRECTIONS: Find the 16 words below in the grid. The words in the grid may be forward, backward, down, up, or diagonal. Each word will always be in a straight line. When you find the word, circle the letters.

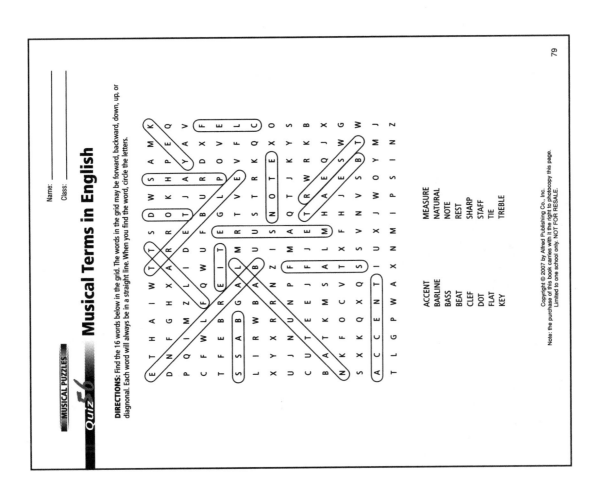

ACCENT
BARLINE
BASS
BEAT
CLEF
DOT
FLAT
KEY

MEASURE
NATURAL
NOTE
REST
SHARP
STAFF
TIE
TREBLE

Quiz 8 — Musical Tempo Terms

Name: _____
Class: _____

DIRECTIONS: Find the 12 words below in the grid. The words in the grid may be forward, backward, down, up, or diagonal. Each word will always be in a straight line. When you find the word, circle the letters.

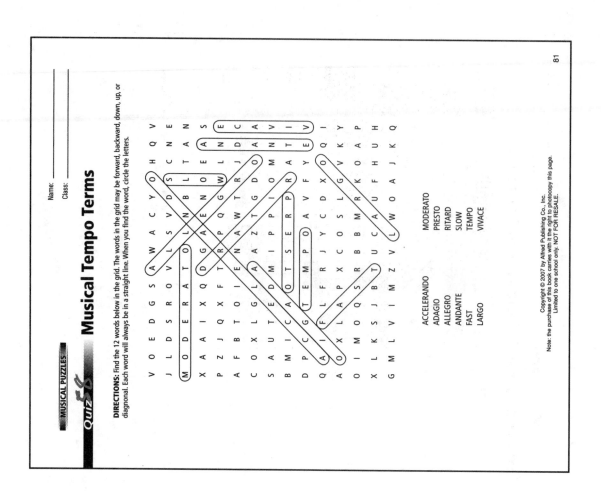

ACCELERANDO	MODERATO
ADAGIO	PRESTO
ALLEGRO	RITARD
ANDANTE	SLOW
FAST	TEMPO
LARGO	VIVACE

Quiz 7 — Musical Terms in Italian

Name: _____
Class: _____

DIRECTIONS: Find the 12 words below in the grid. The words in the grid may be forward, backward, down, up, or diagonal. Each word will always be in a straight line. When you find the word, circle the letters.

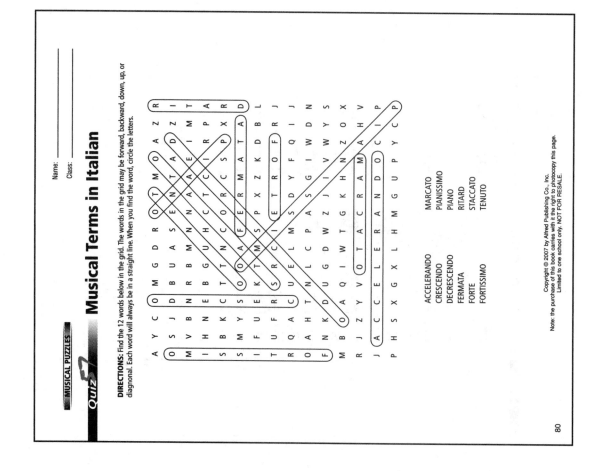

ACCELERANDO	MARCATO
CRESCENDO	PIANISSIMO
DECRESCENDO	PIANO
FERMATA	RITARD
FORTE	STACCATO
FORTISSIMO	TENUTO

Page 82

MUSICAL PUZZLES

Quiz 59 Crossword: The Basics of Music

Name: _____
Class: _____

ACROSS

1. It divides two measures
6. Musical symbol which raises a note a half step
8. Not stop
9. What we do with food
10. Short for Sidney
11. Before noon
12. Musical symbol which lowers a note a half step
14. Treble and bass are this
15. The middle of a donut
17. Notes are in this on a staff
18. Note equal to two eighths
22. Abbr. for Nebraska
23. Santa's helper
24. One of five on your foot
27. Whole, half, quarter, and eighth are this
30. Note equal to two half notes
31. The notes and rests between two barlines; a unit of music

DOWN

1. The lowest male singing voice; also, a clef
2. What we do with a book
3. Note equal to one half of a quarter
4. Type of clef, not the bass
5. Notes are on this...lines and spaces
7. Hello
13. Notes are on this on a staff
14. Not dirty
16. Note equal to two quarters notes
17. To look
19. Silence in music
20. Short for Edward
21. Not one
25. To heal
26. Placed after a note, it means to add half to note's value
28. Hello in Spanish
29. Australian bird that can't fly
30. Us

82

Page 83

MUSICAL PUZZLES

Quiz 60 Crossword: Musical Terms

Name: _____
Class: _____

ACROSS

1. Musical term for soft
3. Abbr. for United States of America
6. After noon
9. Sick
10. Gradually increase in volume
11. Italian musical term meaning very slow tempo
12. To wager
13. Short for Ronald
14. Line above or below a note meaning to hold a note for its full value
15. Dynamite!
17. Short for Susan
18. One plus one
19. Abbr. for cresecendo
22. Musical symbol indicating that a note should be held for more than its normal value
25. Abbr. for Virginia
26. Musical term meaning loud
27. Abbr. for Pennsylvania
28. Musical term meaning to slow the tempo
30. Roman garment
31. Abbreviation for Oregon
32. Not dry
33. Abbr. for mister
37. Abbr. for Tennessee
38. Musical term meaning medium; _____ forte
39. _____ In a moderate tempo

DOWN

1. Politically correct, or personal computer
2. Musical symbol meaning to emphasize a note
4. Italian musical term meaning a cheerful or fast tempo
5. Italian musical term meaning a moderate, graceful tempo
7. Musical symbol meaning to strongly emphasize a note
10. Corn on the _____
11. Short for Leonard
16. Trick or _____
18. Curved line above or below two notes that combines the duration of the note values
20. Abbr. for San Francisco
21. Italian musical term meaning a very slow tempo
23. Not before
24. Also
25. Italian musical term meaning a lively, quick tempo
27. Italian musical term meaning a very fast tempo
29. Abbr. for Alaska
33. Mother
34. Abbr. for American Automobile Association
35. A wizard came from here
36. Abbr. for Delaware

83

How to Use This Book

The purpose of *60 Music Quizzes for Theory and Reading,* is to provide music teachers with an assessment tool for student progress in the areas of music theory and music reading. This book assumes that the basic elements of music theory and music reading have been presented to students. It can be used as an assessment tool no matter what theory or reading methods or texts are used by the teacher. Many theory methods and texts provide at least some evaluation/assessment tools in the form of tests, quizzes, or student workbooks. *60 Music Quizzes for Theory and Reading* can be used to supplement those tests and quizzes. Or it can be used on its own by the teacher who presents music theory and music reading independently of a specific method or book.

This book may also be used as a supplement to *Ready to Read Music: Sequential Lessons in Music Reading Readiness* by Jay Althouse (Alfred Publishing Co., Inc. #21835). *Ready to Read Music* is a fully reproducible book which presents the fundamentals of music reading and the symbols of music in a sequential series.

60 Music Quizzes for Theory and Reading is fully reproducible. Teacher Answer Pages are provided, beginning on page 86, for ease of grading.

About the Author

Jay Althouse received a B.S. degree in Music Education and an M.Ed. degree in Music from Indiana University of Pennsylvania, from which he received the school's Distinguished Alumni award in 2004. For eight years he served as a rights and licenses administrator for a major educational music publisher. During that time he served a term on the Executive Board of the Music Publishers Association of America.

As a composer of choral music, Mr. Althouse has over 500 works in print for choirs of all levels. He is a writer member of ASCAP and is a regular recipient of the ASCAP Special Award for his compositions in the area of standard music.

Mr. Althouse has also co-written several musicals and cantatas with his wife, Sally K. Albrecht, and also compiled and arranged a number of highly regarded vocal solo collections, including most of the *"...for Solo Singers"* series. He is the co-writer, with Russell Robinson, of the best-selling book *The Complete Choral Warm-Up Book*, and, with Judith O'Reilly, a music history/appreciation text entitled *Accent on Composers*. Most recently, he completed a reproducible sequential text on music reading readiness entitled *Ready to Read Music: Sequential Lessons in Music Reading Readiness*. All are available from Alfred Publishing Company.